Ready, Set, Go!®

D1397889

HSPA

Mathematics

3rd Edition

Mel Friedman, M.S.

and the Staff of
Research & Education Association

Research & Education Association

Research & Education Association
61 Ethel Road West
Piscataway, New Jersey 08854
E-mail: info@rea.com

Ready, Set, Go!®
New Jersey HSPA in Mathematics

Printed in the United States of America

Library of Congress Control Number 2009940783

ISBN-13: 978-0-7386-0692-7
ISBN-10: 0-7386-0692-8

A Message to Educators and Students

All New Jersey students are required to pass all sections of the HSPA before they can graduate high school. The state-administered Alternate Proficiency Assessment may be used to evaluate whether or not a student has attained proficiency in the necessary skills if he or she does not pass the HSPA.

The HSPA is not an easy test to pass. It was designed to be more challenging than the state's previous high school exit exam, the HSPT.

It is important, therefore, that students extensively review the subjects covered by the HSPA, and become well acquainted with the types of questions that can be expected to be on the test.

This book is arranged to help students pass the Mathematics section of the HSPA by providing:

1. An individual study plan and guidance to help students concentrate on subject areas that they need to work on most when preparing for the exam.

2. **Four** full-length practice exams based on the format of the most recent exams given. Two exams are printed in this book and two additional exams are available online at *www.rea.com/HSPA*.

3. Types of questions likely to be on the exam.

4. A **full and detailed explanation** of the answer to each exam question.

5. Comprehensive reviews of all subjects covered on the exam.

NOTE TO EDUCATORS:

A large number of class and homework assignments that may be assigned to students are included at the back of the book. Answers to the assigned questions are given in the Teacher's Guide, which is available from REA.

CONTENTS

About Research & Education Association

Founded in 1959, Research & Education Association (REA) is dedicated to publishing the finest and most effective educational materials—including software, study guides, and test preps—for students in elementary school, middle school, high school, college, graduate school, and beyond.

Today REA's wide-ranging catalog is a leading resource for teachers, students, and professionals.

We invite you to visit us at www.rea.com to find out how "REA is making the world smarter."

Acknowledgments

In addition to our authors, we would like to thank Larry B. Kling, Vice President, Editorial, for his overall direction; Pam Weston, Vice President, Publishing, for setting the quality standards for production integrity and managing the publication to completion; Diane Goldschmidt and Alice Leonard, Senior Editors, for coordinating revisions; Rachel DiMatteo, Graphic Designer, for typesetting revisions; and Wende Solano, for typesetting the manuscript.

INDEPENDENT STUDY SCHEDULE
HSPA IN MATHEMATICS

The following study schedule will help you become thoroughly prepared for the HSPA in Mathematics. Although the schedule is designed as a six-week study program, it can be condensed into three weeks if less time is available by collapsing each two-week period into a single week. If you are not enrolled in a structured course, be sure to set aside enough time—at least two hours each day—to study. Keep in mind that the more time you devote to studying for the HSPA in Mathematics, the more prepared and confident you will be on the day of the exam.

Week	Activity
1	Read and study the Cluster I section of the Review. Be sure to thoroughly work all the exercises and problems. If you have particular trouble with any of the questions, go back and study the corresponding section of the review.
2	Read and study the Cluster II section of the Review, and complete all the problems. If you have particular trouble with any of the questions, review that section again.
3	Read and study the Cluster III section of the Review, and complete all the problems. If you have particular trouble with any of the questions, review that section again.
4	Read and study the Cluster IV section of the Review, and complete all the problems. If you have particular trouble with any of the questions, review that section again.
5	Take Practice Tests 1 and 2 printed in this book. After scoring your exam, carefully review the explanations to the questions you missed. If there are any types of questions that are particularly difficult for you, review the relevant subjects by going over the appropriate section.
6	In the final week before your test access the two unique practice tests on line at *www.rea.com/HSPA*. Use the review chapters in this book to study any mathematical topics that are still giving your difficulty.

NEW JERSEY

HSPA

High School Proficiency Assessment in

Mathematics

Passing the New Jersey HSPA in Mathematics

PASSING THE NEW JERSEY HSPA IN MATHEMATICS

ABOUT THIS BOOK AND BONUS ONLINE TESTS

This book will provide you with an accurate and complete representation of the New Jersey High School Proficiency Assessment (HSPA) in Mathematics. Inside you will find subject reviews that are designed to provide you with the information and strategies needed to do well on this section of the HSPA. Four complete practice tests are provided: two printed in this book and two additional unique tests online at *www.rea.com/HSPA*. All of the tests are based on the official HSPA. REA's practice tests contain every type of question that you can expect to encounter on the HSPA. Following each model test, you will find an answer key with detailed explanations designed to help you completely understand the test material. (Note to educators: Also included are over 200 class and homework problems that can be assigned to students. Answers to these questions can be found in the Teacher's Guide, which is available from REA.)

ABOUT THE TEST

Who takes the test and what is it used for?

The HSPA is mandatory for New Jersey high school juniors. It gauges students' knowledge and skills in the New Jersey Core Curriculum Content Standards for reading, writing, and mathematics.

All New Jersey high school students are required to pass the entire test in order to graduate. Students who do not pass a section are given an opportunity to retake the test in the fall or spring of the 12th grade.

Who administers the test?

The HSPA was developed and is administered by the New Jersey State Department of Education and involves the assistance of educators throughout the state. The test development process is designed and implemented to ensure that the content and difficulty level of the test are appropriate.

When and where is the test given?

The HSPA Math and English tests are administered in March and October. They are given at all public high schools. The testing lasts for three days, and may be taken on alternate days if a conflict—such as a religious obligation—exists.

To receive information on upcoming administrations of the HSPA, consult the Grade 11 High School Proficiency Assessment Parent Information Bulletin. The bulletin can be obtained from your guidance counselor or by contacting:

New Jersey State Department of Education
P.O. Box 500
Trenton, NJ 08625
Phone: (609) 292-4469
Website: www.state.nj.us/education

Is there a registration fee?

No. Because all New Jersey high school students are required to take this test, no fee is imposed.

HOW TO USE THIS BOOK

What do I study first?

Read over the reviews and the suggestions for test taking. Studying the reviews thoroughly will reinforce the basic skills you will need to do well on the test. Be sure to take the practice tests to become familiar with the format and procedures involved with taking the actual HSPA in Mathematics.

To best utilize your study time, follow our HSPA Independent Study Schedule, located in the front of this book. Brushing up on the areas you did well on wouldn't hurt, either.

When should I start studying?

It is never too early to start studying for the HSPA. The earlier you begin, the more time you will have to sharpen your skills. Do not procrastinate! Cramming is *not* an effective way to study, since it does not allow you the time needed to learn the test material. The sooner you learn the format of the exam, the more time you will have to familiarize yourself with the exam content.

FORMAT OF THE HSPA IN MATHEMATICS

Each section of the HSPA in Mathematics contains 10 multiple-choice questions and 2 open-ended questions. For the multiple-choice questions, you are offered four answer options. The open-ended questions call for you to write a short answer, so you are not presented with answer choices. After each section of the test, you are given a brief break.

Mathematics Content Clusters

In the mathematics sections, you will encounter questions on the following "clusters" of knowledge:

- Number Sense, Concepts, and Applications—These questions deal with the following topics: our numeration system (and its application in real-world situations); and ratios, percents, and proportions.

- Spatial Sense and Geometry—These questions deal with the following topics: identifying geometric properties, relationships, and patterns in real-world and/or problem-solving situations; using coordinate geometry and principles of congruence, similarity, and transformations; and direct and indirect measurement.

- Data Analysis, Probability, Statistics, and Discrete Mathematics—These questions deal with the following topics: probabilities of simple and compound events; statistical distributions; organization and representation of data; discrete mathematics; and iterative and recursive processes.

- Patterns, Functions, and Algebra—These questions test the student's capability in the following topics: patterns and inductive reasoning; various types of functions; and algebraic concepts and processes.

CALCULATOR USE

Calculators will be permitted and, in fact, will be provided during the test. You may use a programmable or non-programmable four-function, scientific, or graphing calculator. No pocket organizers, hand-held mini-computers, paper tape, or noisy calculators may be used. In addition, calculators requiring an external power source will not be permitted. You will not be allowed to share a calculator.

ABOUT THE REVIEW SECTION

The reviews in this book are designed to help you sharpen the basic skills needed to approach the HSPA, as well as to provide strategies for attacking each type of question. You will also find exercises to reinforce what you have learned. By using the reviews in conjunction with the practice tests, you will put yourself in a position to master the HSPA.

The Mathematics Section Review covers the basics of what you need to know to pass the Mathematics Section of the HSPA. You will find strategies for the Mathematics Section, a review of each cluster and its individual "macros," and exercises to strengthen your abilities in these areas.

ABOUT YOUR SCORE

When you take the HSPA, your scores will be reported as being in one of three proficiency levels—Advanced Proficient, Proficient, or Partially Proficient. Subtotal scores will also be reported for the specific knowledge and skills measured in each content area. The following information can be used in determining whether you have passed the practice tests provided in this book.

For each section, there is a possible number of points that a student can receive. Each multiple-choice question equals 1 point, and each open-ended question is worth from 0 to 3 points. To determine points received, the student must add up all correct responses for the multiple-choice and open-ended questions.

When the scoring is done for open-ended questions in the Mathematics sections, the number of points received is established by an evaluator. Each evaluator is specially trained for this type of test response.

Once the sections are graded, the points received are added together to determine the raw score.

Your score will be scaled to account for differences in various test administrations and forms; the scaled Mathematics score will be within a range of 100 to 300 points, with 200 being the minimum passing ("Proficient") score.

How Do I Score My Practice Test?

Use the scoring worksheet below to score each of our two practice tests. (It is advised that a teacher review and score all open-ended questions.) While the score you earn on our practice tests approximates the score you will receive on the HSPA, it should not be construed as a precise predictor of your actual test performance. While it is not possible to replicate the scaling formula for the HSPA, and the raw score that represents a passing score differs from year to year, please note that for the two Practice Tests in this book, a raw score of approximately 33 will equate with a passing (Proficient) score.

_____	+	_____	=	_____
Part I points received multiple-choice		Part I points received open-ended		Part I raw score

_____	+	_____	=	_____
Part II points received multiple-choice		Part II points received open-ended		Part II raw score

_____	+	_____	=	_____
Part III points received multiple-choice		Part III points received open-ended		Part III raw score

_____	+	_____	=	_____
Part IV points received multiple-choice		Part IV points received open-ended		Part IV raw score

_____

Total raw score

TEST-TAKING TIPS

Although you may not be familiar with standardized tests such as the HSPA, there are many ways to acquaint yourself with this type of examination and help alleviate your test-taking anxieties. Listed below are ways to help you become accustomed to the HSPA, some of which may be applied to other standardized tests as well.

Become comfortable with the format of the HSPA. When you are practicing, simulate the conditions under which you will be taking the actual test. Stay calm and pace yourself. After simulating the test only a couple of times, you will boost your chances of doing well, and you will be able to sit for the actual HSPA with much more confidence.

Read all of the possible answers. Just because you think you have found the correct response, do not automatically assume that it is the best answer. Read through each choice to be sure that you are not making a mistake by jumping to conclusions.

Use the process of elimination. Go through each answer to a question and eliminate as many of the answer choices as possible. By eliminating two answer choices, you can vastly improve your chances of getting the item correct, since there will only be two or three choices left from which to make your guess. Guess only if you can eliminate at least two answers, as wrong answers will be penalized.

Work quickly and steadily. You will have only minutes to work on each section, so work quickly and steadily to avoid focusing on any one problem for too long. Taking the practice tests in this book will help you learn to budget your precious time.

Learn the directions and format for each section of the test. Familiarizing yourself with the directions and format of the different test sections will not only save time, but will also help you avoid anxiety (and the mistakes caused by getting anxious).

Work on the easier questions first. If you find yourself working too long on one question, make a mark next to it on your test booklet and continue. After you have answered all of the questions that you can, go back to the ones you have skipped.

Be sure that the answer oval you are marking corresponds to the number of the question in the test booklet. Since the multiple-choice sections are graded by machine, marking one wrong answer can throw off your answer key and your score. Be extremely careful.

Eliminate obvious wrong answers. Sometimes an HSPA question will have one or two answer choices that are a little odd. These answers will be obviously wrong for one of three reasons: (1) they may be impossible given the conditions of the problem, (2) they may violate mathematical rules or principles, or (3) they may be illogical. Being able to spot obvious wrong answers before you finish a problem gives you an advantage because you will be able to make a more educated guess from the remaining choices even if you are unable to fully solve the problem.

Work from answer choices. One of the ways you can use a multiple-choice format to your advantage is to work backwards from the answer choices to solve a problem. This is not a strategy you can use all of the time, but it can be helpful if you can just plug the choices into a given statement or equation. The answer choices can often narrow the scope of responses. You may be able to make an educated guess based on eliminating choices that you know do not fit into the problem.

THE DAY OF THE TEST

Before the Test

On the day of the test, you should wake up early (it is hoped after a decent night's rest) and have a good breakfast. Make sure to dress comfortably, so that you are not distracted by being too hot or too cold while taking the test. Also plan to arrive at school on time. This will allow you to collect your thoughts and relax before the test, and will also spare you the anguish that comes with being late.

If you would like, you may wear a watch to school. However, you may not wear one that makes noise, because it may disturb the other test takers. Only your pencils and calculator will be permitted into the testing area. You will be provided with a Mathematics Reference Sheet, containing a ruler, useful formulas, geometric shapes, and various information that may be useful in solving problems. Calculators will also be provided, as well as pencils.

During the Test

Follow all of the rules and instructions given by your teacher or the test supervisor. If you do not, you risk being dismissed from the test and having your HSPA scores canceled.

When all of the test materials have been passed out, the test supervisor will give you directions for filling out your answer folder. You must fill out this sheet carefully since this information will be printed on your score report. Fill out your name exactly as it appears on your identification documents, unless otherwise instructed.

Remember that you can write in your test booklet, as no scratch paper will be provided. Mark your answers in the appropriate spaces in the answer folder. Each numbered row will contain four ovals corresponding to each answer choice for that question. Fill in the oval that corresponds to your answer darkly, completely, and neatly. You can change your answer, but be sure to completely erase your old answer. Only one answer should be marked. This is very important, as your answer sheet will be machine-scored and stray lines or unnecessary marks may cause the machine to score your answers incorrectly.

NEW JERSEY

HSPA

High School Proficiency Assessment in
Mathematics

CHAPTER 1

Review of Cluster I: Number Sense, Concepts, and Applications

Cluster I, Macro A

Integers and Real Numbers

Most of the numbers used in algebra belong to a set called the **real numbers** or **reals**. This set can be represented graphically by the real number line.

Given the number line below, we arbitrarily fix a point and label it with the number 0. In a similar manner, we can label any point on the line with one of the real numbers, depending on its position relative to 0. Numbers to the right of 0 are positive, while those to the left are negative. Value increases from left to right, so that if *a* is to the right of *b*, it is said to be greater than *b*.

If we now divide the number line into equal segments, we can label the points on this line with real numbers. For example, the point two lengths to the left of 0 is –2, while the point three lengths to the right of 0 is +3 (the + sign is usually assumed, so +3 is written simply as 3). The number line now looks like this:

These boundary points represent the subset of the reals known as the **integers**. The set of integers is made up of both the positive and negative whole numbers:

$$\{\ldots, -4, -3, -2, -1, 0, 1, 2, 3, 4, \ldots\}.$$

Some subsets of integers are:

Natural Numbers or Positive Integers—the set of integers starting with 1 and increasing:

$$N = \{1, 2, 3, 4, \ldots\}.$$

Whole Numbers—the set of integers starting with 0 and increasing:

$$W = \{0, 1, 2, 3, \ldots\}.$$

Negative Integers—the set of integers starting with –1 and decreasing:

$$Z = \{-1, -2, -3, \ldots\}.$$

Prime Numbers—the set of positive integers greater than 1 that are divisible only by 1 and themselves:

$$\{2, 3, 5, 7, 11, \ldots\}.$$

Even Integers—the set of integers divisible by 2:

$$\{\ldots, -4, -2, 0, 2, 4, 6, \ldots\}.$$

Odd Integers—the set of integers not divisible by 2:

$$\{\ldots, -3, -1, 1, 3, 5, 7, \ldots\}.$$

Absolute Value

The absolute value of a number is indicated by two vertical lines around the number. The absolute value is always greater than or equal to zero.

The absolute value of a real number A is defined as follows:

$$|A| = \begin{cases} A, & \text{if } A \geq 0 \\ -A, & \text{if } A < 0 \end{cases}$$

Example

$$|5| = 5, |-8| = -(-8) = 8$$

Absolute values follow the given rules:

(A) $|-A| = |A|$

(B) $|A| \geq 0$, equality holding only if $A = 0$

(C) $\left|\dfrac{A}{B}\right| = \dfrac{|A|}{|B|}, B \neq 0$

(D) $|AB| = |A| \times |B|$

(E) $|A|^2 = A^2$

Absolute value can also be expressed on the real number line as the distance from the point represented by the real number to the point labeled 0.

The example below illustrates | −3 |.

3 unit lengths

Exponents

When a number is multiplied by itself a specific number of times, it is said to be **raised to a power**. The way this is written is $a^n = b$, where a is the number or **base**, n is the **exponent** or **power** that indicates the number of times the base is to be multiplied by itself, and b is the product of this multiplication.

In the expression 3^2, 3 is the base and 2 is the exponent. This means that 3 is multiplied by itself 2 times and the product is 9.

An exponent can be either positive or negative. A negative exponent implies a fraction. If n is a positive number, then

$$a^{-n} = \frac{1}{a^n}, a \neq 0. \text{ So, } 2^{-4} = \frac{1}{2^4} = \frac{1}{16}.$$

An exponent of 0 gives a result of 1, assuming that the base is not equal to 0.

$$a^0 = 1, a \neq 0$$

An exponent can also be a fraction. If m and n are positive integers,

$$a^{\frac{m}{n}} = \sqrt[n]{a^m}.$$

The numerator remains the exponent of a, but the denominator tells what root to take. For example,

(1) $4^{\frac{3}{2}} = \sqrt[2]{4^3} = \sqrt{64} = 8$ (2) $3^{\frac{4}{2}} = \sqrt[2]{3^4} = \sqrt{81} = 9$

If a fractional exponent were negative, the same operation would take place, but the result would be a fraction. For example,

(1) $27^{-\frac{2}{3}} = \frac{1}{27^{2/3}} = \frac{1}{\sqrt[3]{27^2}} = \frac{1}{\sqrt[3]{729}} = \frac{1}{9}$

PROBLEM

Simplify the following expressions:

(1) -3^{-2}

(3) $\dfrac{-3}{4^{-1}}$

(2) $(-3)^{-2}$

SOLUTION

(1) Here the exponent applies only to 3. Since

$$x^{-y} = \frac{1}{x^y}, \; -3^{-2} = -(3)^{-2} = -\frac{1}{3^2} = -\frac{1}{9}$$

(2) In this case the exponent applies to the negative base. Thus,

$$(-3)^{-2} = \frac{1}{(-3)^2} = \frac{1}{(-3)(-3)} = \frac{1}{9}$$

(3) $\dfrac{-3}{4^{-1}} = \dfrac{-3}{\left(\dfrac{1}{4}\right)^1} = \dfrac{-3}{\dfrac{1^1}{4^1}} = \dfrac{-3}{\dfrac{1}{4}}$

Division by a fraction is equivalent to multiplication by that fraction's reciprocal, thus

$$\frac{-3}{\dfrac{1}{4}} = -3 \times \frac{4}{1} = -12, \text{ so } \frac{-3}{4^{-1}} = -12$$

General Laws of Exponents

A) $a^p a^q = a^{p+q}$

$4^2 4^3 = 4^{2+3} = 4^5 = 1{,}024$

B) $(a^p)^q = a^{pq}$

$(2^3)^2 = 2^6 = 64$

C) $\dfrac{a^p}{a^q} = a^{p-q}$

$$\frac{3^6}{3^2} = 3^4 = 81$$

D) $(ab)^p = a^p b^p$

$$(3 \times 2)^2 = 3^2 \times 2^2 = (9)(4) = 36$$

E) $\left(\dfrac{a}{b}\right)^p = \dfrac{a^p}{b^p}, b \neq 0$

$$\left(\frac{4}{5}\right)^2 = \frac{4^2}{5^2} = \frac{16}{25}$$

Exercise: Exponents

Multiplication

> **DIRECTIONS:** Simplify the following expressions.

1. $2^2 \times 2^5 \times 2^3 =$

    (A) 2^{10} (B) 4^{10} (C) 8^{10} (D) 2^{30}

2. $a^4 b^2 \times a^3 b =$

    (A) ab (B) $2a^7 b^2$ (C) $2a^{12}b$ (D) $a^7 b^3$

3. $m^8 n^3 \times m^2 n \times m^4 n^2 =$

    (A) $3m^{16}n^6$ (B) $m^{14}n^6$ (C) $3m^{14}n^5$ (D) $3m^{14}n^5$

> **DIRECTIONS:** Simplify the following expressions.

4. $11^8 \div 11^5 =$

    (A) 1^3 (B) 11^3 (C) 11^{13} (D) 11^{40}

5. $x^{10}y^8 \div x^7 y^3 =$

    (A) $x^2 y^5$ (B) $x^3 y^4$ (C) $x^3 y^5$ (D) $x^2 y^4$

6. $a^{14} \div a^9 =$

    (A) 1^5 (B) a^5 (C) $2a^5$ (D) a^{23}

Power to a Power

> **DIRECTIONS:** Simplify the following expressions.

7. $(3^6)^2 =$

    (A) 3^4 (B) 3^8 (C) 3^{12} (D) 9^6

8. $(r^3 p^6)^3 =$

    (A) $r^9 p^{18}$ (B) $(rp)^{12}$ (C) $r^6 p^9$ (D) $3r^3 p^6$

9. $(m^6 n^5 q^3)^2 =$

    (A) $2m^6 n^5 q^3$ (B) $m^4 n^3 q$ (C) $m^8 n^7 q^5$ (D) $m^{12} n^{10} q^6$

A **relation R** describes a given rule or operation for a set of numbers. If aRa, then R is reflexive for all numbers which are denoted as a.

The symbol = has a reflexive property, since **a=a**. The symmetric property states: If aRb, then bRa, for all a, b. The symbol = is symmetric because if a=b, then b=a. The transitive property states: If aRb and bRc, then aRc. Once again, the = symbol is transitive, since if a=b and b=c, then a=c. Any relation R that is reflexive, symmetric, and transitive is called an equivalence relation. Thus "=" is an equivalence relation.

An example of a relation which is not an equivalence relation is "<," because a<a is false. Also, if a<b, then b<a is false.

The Associative Law of Addition: a+(b+c) = (a+b)+c for all a, b, c.

The Associative Law of Multiplication: (a)(bc) = (ab)c for all a, b, c.

The Commutative Law of Addition: a+b = b+a, for all a, b.

The Commutative Law of Multiplication: ab = ba, for all a, b.

The Distributive Law of Addition over Multiplication: (a)(b+c) = ab + ac, for all a, b, c.

Cluster I, Macro B

Ratios and Proportions

The ratio of two numbers x and y written $x : y$ is the fraction x/y where $y \neq 0$. A ratio compares x to y by dividing one by the other. Therefore, in order to compare ratios, simply compare the fractions.

A proportion is an equality of two ratios. The laws of proportion are listed below:

If $a/b = c/d$, then

$ad = bc$

$b/a = d/c$

$a/c = b/d$

PROBLEM

Solve the proportion $\dfrac{x+1}{4} = \dfrac{15}{12}$.

SOLUTION

Cross-multiply to determine x; that is, multiply the numerator of the first fraction by the denominator of the second, and equate this to the product of the numerator of the second and the denominator of the first.

$$(x + 1)\, 12 = 4 \times 15$$
$$12x + 12 = 60$$
$$12x = 48$$
$$x = 4$$

Exercise: Ratios and Proportions

DIRECTIONS: Simplify the following expressions.

1. Solve for n: $\dfrac{2}{3} = \dfrac{n}{72}$

   (A) 12   (B) 48   (C) 64   (D) 56

2. A class of 24 students contains 16 males. What is the ratio of females to males?

   (A) $1 : 2$ (B) $2 : 1$ (C) $2 : 3$ (D) $3 : 1$

3. In a survey by mail, 30 out of 750 questionnaires were returned. Write the ratio of questionnaires returned to questionnaires mailed (write in simplest form).

   (A) $1 : 25$ (B) $24 : 25$ (C) $1 : 24$ (D) $1 : 4$

Rate

One of the formulas you will use for rate problems will be

$$\text{Rate} \times \text{Time} = \text{Distance}$$

PROBLEM

> If a plane travels five hours from New York to California at a speed of 600 miles per hour, how many miles does the plane travel?

SOLUTION

Using the formula rate × time = distance, multiply 600 mph × 5 hours = 3,000 miles.

The average rate at which an object travels can be solved by dividing the total distance traveled by the total amount of time.

PROBLEM

> On a 40-mile bicycle trip, Cathy rode half the distance at 20 mph and the other half at 10 mph. What was Cathy's average speed on the bike trip?

SOLUTION

First you need to break down the problem. On half of the trip which would be 20 miles, Cathy rode 20 mph. Using the rate formula, $^{\text{distance}}/_{\text{rate}} =$ time, you would compute

$$\frac{20 \text{ miles}}{20 \text{ miles per hour}} = 1 \text{ hour}$$

to travel the first 20 miles. During the second 20 miles, Cathy traveled at 10 miles per hour, which would be

$$\frac{20 \text{ miles}}{10 \text{ miles per hour}} = 2 \text{ hours}$$

Thus, the average speed Cathy traveled would be $^{40}/_3 = 13.3$ miles per hour.

In solving for some rate problems you can use cross-multiplication involving ratios to solve for *x*.

PROBLEM

> If two pairs of shoes cost $52, then what is the cost of ten pairs of shoes at this rate?

SOLUTION

$$\frac{2}{52} = \frac{10}{x}, \; 2x = 52 \times 10, \; x = \frac{520}{2}, \; x = \$260$$

Exercise: Rate

> **DIRECTIONS:** Solve to find the rate.

1. Two towns are 420 miles apart. A car leaves the first town traveling toward the second town at 55 mph. At the same time, a second car leaves the second town and heads toward the first town at 65 mph. How long will it take for the two cars to meet?

    (A) 2 hr   (B) 3 hr   (C) 3.5 hr   (D) 4 hr

2. A camper leaves the campsite walking due east at a rate of 3.5 mph. Another camper leaves the campsite at the same time but travels due west. In two hours the two campers will be 15 miles apart. What is the walking rate of the second camper?

    (A) 4 mph   (B) 3 mph   (C) 3.25 mph   (D) 3.5 mph

3. A bicycle racer covers a 75-mile training route to prepare for an upcoming race. If the racer could increase his speed by 5 mph, he could complete the same course in $^3/_4$ of the time. Find his average rate of speed.

    (A) 15 mph   (B) 15.5 mph   (C) 16 mph   (D) 18 mph

Discount

If the discount problem asks for the final price after the discount, first multiply the original price by the percent of discount. Then subtract this result from the original price.

If the problem asks for the original price when only the percent of discount and the discounted price are given, simply subtract the percent of discount from 100% and divide this percent into the sale price. This will give you the original price.

PROBLEM

> A popular bookstore gives 10% discount to students. What does a student actually pay for a book costing $24?

SOLUTION

10% of $24 is $2.40 and hence the student pays $24 − $2.40 = $21.60.

PROBLEM

> Eugene paid $100 for a business suit. The suit's price included a 25% discount. What was the original price of the suit?

SOLUTION

Let x represent the original price of the suit and take the complement of .25 (discount price) which is .75.

$$.75x = \$100 \text{ or } x = \$133.33$$

So, the original price of the suit is $133.33.

Exercise: Discount

> **DIRECTIONS:** Find cost, price, or discount as appropriate.

1. A man bought a coat marked 20% off for $156. How much had the coat cost originally?

   (A) $136   (B) $156   (C) $175   (D) $195

2. A woman saved $225 on the new sofa which was on sale for 30% off. What was the original price of the sofa?

   (A) $25   (B) $200   (C) $750   (D) $525

3. At an office supply store, customers are given a discount if they pay in cash. If a customer is given a discount of $9.66 on a total order of $276, what is the percent of discount?

   (A) 2%   (B) 3.5%   (C) 4.5%   (D) 9.66%

NEW JERSEY

HSPA

High School Proficiency Assessment in

Mathematics

CHAPTER 2

Review of Cluster II: Spatial Sense and Geometry

Cluster II, Macro A

Geometry

Points, Lines, and Angles

Geometry is built upon a series of undefined terms. These terms are those which we accept as known in order to define other undefined terms.

A) **Point**: Although we represent points on paper with small dots, a point has no size, thickness, or width.

B) **Line**: A line is a series of adjacent points which extends indefinitely. A line can be either curved or straight; however, unless otherwise stated, the term "line" refers to a straight line.

C) **Plane**: A plane is a collection of points lying on a flat surface, which extends indefinitely in all directions.

If A and B are two points on a line, then the **line segment** AB is the set of points on that line between A and B and including A and B, which are endpoints. The line segment is referred to as $\overline{AB}$.

A **ray** is a series of points that lie to one side of a single endpoint.

PROBLEM

How many lines can be found that contain

(1) one given point?   (2) two given points?

(3) three given points?

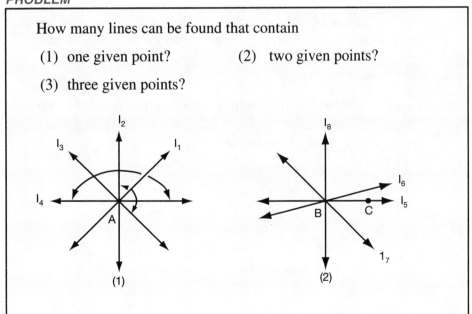

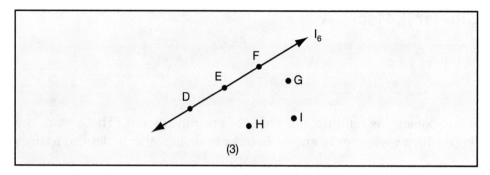

(3)

SOLUTION

(1) *Given one point A,* there are an infinite number of distinct lines that contain the given point. To see this, consider line l_1 passing through point A. By rotating l_1 around A like the hands of a clock, we obtain different lines l_2, l_3, etc. Since we can rotate l_1 in infinitely many ways, there are infinitely many lines containing A.

(2) *Given two distinct points B and C,* there is one and only one distinct line. To see this, consider all the lines containing point B; l_5, l_6, l_7, and l_8. Only l_5 contains both points B and C. Thus, there is only one line containing both points B and C. Since there is always at least one line containing two distinct points and never more than one, the line passing through the two points is said to be determined by the two points.

(3) *Given three distinct points,* there may be one line or none. If a line exists that contains the three points, such as D, E, and F, then the points are said to be *collinear.* If no such line exists — as in the case of points G, H, and I, then the points are said to be noncollinear.

Intersecting Lines and Angles

An **angle** is a collection of points which is the union of two rays having the same endpoint. An angle such as the one illustrated below can be referred to in any of the following ways:

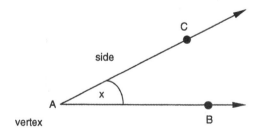

A) by a capital letter which names its vertex, i.e., $\angle A$;

B) by a lowercase letter or number placed inside the angle, i.e., $\angle x$;

C) by three capital letters, where the middle letter is the vertex and the other two letters are not on the same ray, i.e., $\angle CAB$ or $\angle BAC$, both of which represent the angle illustrated in the figure.

Types of Angles

A) **Vertical angles** are formed when two lines intersect. These opposite angles are equal.

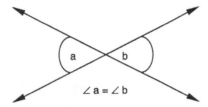

B) **Adjacent angles** are two angles with a common vertex and a common side, but no common interior points. In the following figure, $\angle DAC$ and $\angle BAC$ are adjacent angles. $\angle DAB$ and $\angle BAC$ are not.

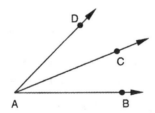

C) A **right angle** is an angle whose measure is 90°.

D) An **acute angle** is an angle whose measure is larger than 0° but less than 90°.

E) An **obtuse angle** is an angle whose measure is larger than 90° but less than 180°.

F) A **straight angle** is an angle whose measure is 180°. Such an angle is, in fact, a straight line.

G) A **reflex angle** is an angle whose measure is greater than 180° but less than 360°.

H) **Complementary angles** are two angles, the sum of the measures of which equals 90°.

I)   **Supplementary angles** are two angles, the sum of the measures of which equals 180°.

J)   **Congruent angles** are angles of equal measure.

PROBLEM

In the figure, we are given $\overline{AB}$ and triangle *ABC*. We are told that the measure of $\angle 1$ is five times the measure of $\angle 2$. Determine the measures of $\angle 1$ and $\angle 2$.

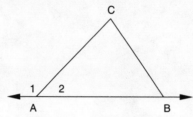

SOLUTION

Since $\angle 1$ and $\angle 2$ are adjacent angles whose non-common sides lie on a straight line, they are, by definition, supplementary. As supplements, their measures must sum to 180°.

If we let x = the measure of $\angle 2$, then $5x$ = the measure of $\angle 1$.

To determine the respective angle measures, set $x + 5x = 180$ and solve for x. $6x = 180$. Therefore, $x = 30$ and $5x = 150$.

Therefore, the measure of $\angle 1 = 150°$ and the measure of $\angle 2 = 30°$.

Perpendicular Lines

Two lines are said to be **perpendicular** if they intersect and form right angles. The symbol for perpendicular (or is therefore perpendicular to) is $\perp$; $\overline{AB}$ is perpendicular to $\overline{CD}$ is written $\overline{AB} \perp \overline{CD}$.

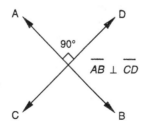

PROBLEM

We are given straight lines $\overleftrightarrow{AB}$ and $\overleftrightarrow{CD}$ intersecting at point *P*. $\overrightarrow{PR}$ $\perp \overleftrightarrow{AB}$ and the measure of $\angle APD$ is 170°. Find the measures of $\angle 1$, $\angle 2$, $\angle 3$, and $\angle 4$. (See figure below.)

SOLUTION

This problem will involve making use of several of the properties of supplementary and vertical angles, as well as perpendicular lines.

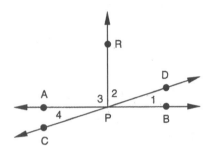

$\angle APD$ and $\angle 1$ are adjacent angles whose non-common sides lie on a straight line, $\overleftrightarrow{AB}$. Therefore, they are supplements and their measures sum to 180°.

$$m \angle APD + m \angle 1 = 180°$$

We know $m \angle APD = 170°$. Therefore, by substitution, $170° + m \angle 1 = 180°$. This implies $m \angle 1 = 10°$. ,

$\angle 1$ and $\angle 4$ are vertical angles because they are formed by the intersection of two straight lines, $\overleftrightarrow{CD}$ and $\overleftrightarrow{AB}$, and their sides form two pairs of opposite rays. As vertical angles, they are, by theorem, of equal measure. Since $m \angle 1 = 10°$, then $m \angle 4 = 10°$.

Since $\overrightarrow{PR} \perp \overleftrightarrow{AB}$, at their intersection the angles formed must be right angles. Therefore, $\angle 3$ is a right angle and its measure is 90°. $m \angle 3 = 90°$.

The figure shows us that $\angle APD$ is composed of $\angle 3$ and $\angle 2$. Since the measure of the whole must be equal to the sum of the measures of its parts, $m \angle APD = m \angle 3 + m \angle 2$. We know the $m \angle APD = 170°$ and $m \angle 3 = 90°$; therefore, by substitution, we can solve for $m \angle 2$, our last unknown.

$$170° = 90° + m \angle 2, \text{ so } m \angle 2 = 170° - 90° = 80°$$

Therefore, $m \angle 1 = 10°$ $m \angle 2 = 80°$

$m \angle 3 = 90°$ $m \angle 4 = 10°$

Parallel Lines

Two lines are called **parallel lines** if, and only if, they are in the same plane (coplanar) and do not intersect. The symbol for parallel, or is parallel to, is ∥; $\overleftrightarrow{AB}$ is parallel to $\overleftrightarrow{CD}$ is written $\overleftrightarrow{AB} \parallel \overleftrightarrow{CD}$.

The distance between two parallel lines is the length of the perpendicular segment from any point on one line to the other line.

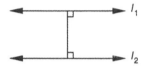

Given a line l and a point P not on line l, there is one and only one line through point P that is parallel to line l.

Two coplanar lines are either intersecting lines or parallel lines.

If two (or more) lines are perpendicular to the same line, then they are parallel to each other.

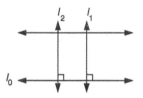

If two lines are cut by a transversal so that alternate interior angles are equal, the lines are parallel.

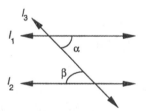

If two lines are parallel to the same line, then they are parallel to each other.

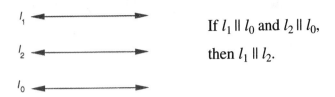

If $l_1 \parallel l_0$ and $l_2 \parallel l_0$,

then $l_1 \parallel l_2$.

If a line is perpendicular to one of two parallel lines, then it is perpendicular to the other line, too.

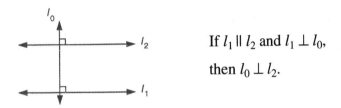

If $l_1 \parallel l_2$ and $l_1 \perp l_0$,

then $l_0 \perp l_2$.

If two lines being cut by a transversal form congruent corresponding angles, then the two lines are parallel.

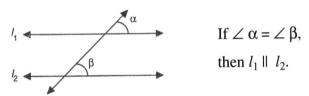

If $\angle\, \alpha = \angle\, \beta$,

then $l_1 \parallel l_2$.

If two lines being cut by a transversal form interior angles on the same side of the transversal that are supplementary, then the two lines are parallel.

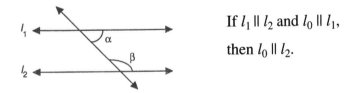

If $l_1 \parallel l_2$ and $l_0 \parallel l_1$,

then $l_0 \parallel l_2$.

If a line is parallel to one of two parallel lines, it is also parallel to the other line.

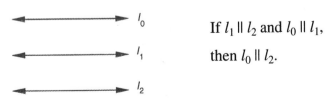

If $l_1 \parallel l_2$ and $l_0 \parallel l_1$,

then $l_0 \parallel l_2$.

If two parallel lines are cut by a transversal, then:

A)   The alternate interior angles are congruent.

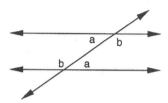

B)   The corresponding angles are congruent.

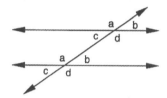

C)   The consecutive (same side) interior angles are supplementary.

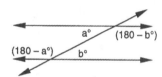

D)   The alternate exterior angles are congruent.

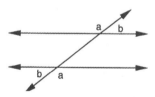

Exercise: Points, Lines, and Angles

DIRECTIONS: Find the appropriate solutions.

Intersecting Lines and Angles

1.   Find *a*.

   (A) 38°   (B) 68°

   (C) 78°   (D) 90°

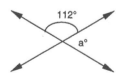

2. Find *c*.

   (A) 32°   (B) 48°

   (C) 58°   (D) 82°

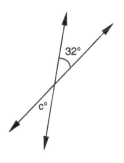

Perpendicular Lines

3. $\overline{BA} \perp \overline{BC}$ and $m \angle DBC = 53°$.
   Find $m \angle ABD$.

   (A) 27°   (B) 33°

   (C) 37°   (D) 53°

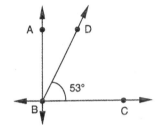

4. If $m \perp p$, which of the following statements is true?

   (A) $\angle 1 \cong \angle 2$

   (B) $\angle 4 \cong \angle 5$

   (C) $m \angle 4 + m \angle 5 > m \angle 1 + m \angle 2$

   (D) $m \angle 3 > m \angle 2$

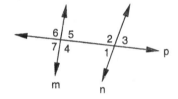

Parallel Lines

5. If $a \parallel b$, find *z*.

   (A) 26°   (B) 32°

   (C) 64°   (D) 86°

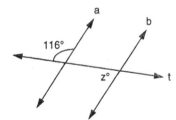

6. If $r \parallel s$, find $m \angle 2$.

   (A) 17°   (B) 73°

   (C) 43°   (D) 67°

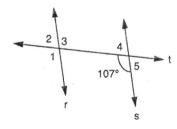

Triangles

A closed three-sided geometric figure is called a **triangle**. The points of the intersection of the sides of a triangle are called the **vertices** of the triangle.

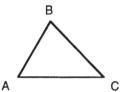

The **perimeter** of a triangle is the sum of the measures of the sides of the triangle.

A triangle with no equal sides is called a **scalene** triangle.

A triangle having at least two equal sides is called an **isosceles** triangle. The third side is called the **base** of the triangle.

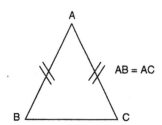

A side of a triangle is a line segment whose endpoints are the vertices of two angles of the triangle.

An interior angle of a triangle is an angle formed by two sides and includes the third side within its collection of points.

An **equilateral triangle** is a triangle having three equal sides. $\overline{AB} = \overline{AC} = \overline{BC}$

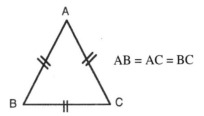

$$AB = AC = BC$$

A triangle with one obtuse angle greater than 90° is called an **obtuse triangle**.

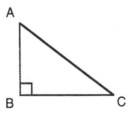

An **acute triangle** is a triangle with three acute angles (less than 90°).

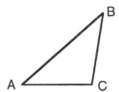

A triangle with a right angle is called a **right triangle**. The side opposite the right angle in a right triangle is called the **hypotenuse** of the right triangle. The other two sides are called arms or legs of the right triangle.

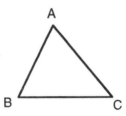

An **altitude** of a triangle is a line segment from a vertex of the triangle perpendicular to the opposite side.

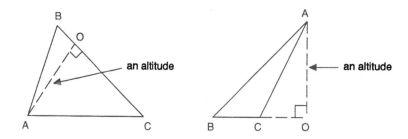

A line segment connecting a vertex of a triangle and the midpoint of the opposite side is called a **median** of the triangle.

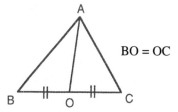

A line that bisects and is perpendicular to a side of a triangle is called a **perpendicular bisector** of that side.

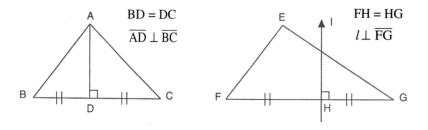

An **angle bisector** of a triangle is a line that bisects an angle and extends to the opposite side of the triangle.

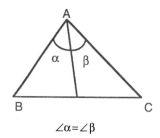

The line segment that joins the midpoints of two sides of a triangle is called a **midline** of the triangle.

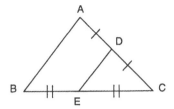

An **exterior angle** of a triangle is an angle formed outside a triangle by one side of the triangle and the extension of an adjacent side.

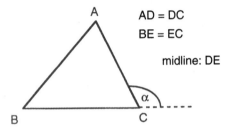

AD = DC

BE = EC

midline: DE

A triangle whose three interior angles have equal measure is said to be equiangular.

Three or more lines (or rays or segments) are **concurrent** if there exists one point common to all of them, that is, if they all intersect at the same point.

PROBLEM

The measure of the vertex angle of an isosceles triangle exceeds the measurement of each base angle by 30°. Find the value of each angle of the triangle.

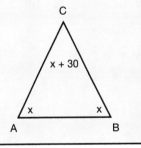

SOLUTION

We know that the sum of the values of the angles of a triangle is 180°. In an isosceles triangle, the angles opposite the congruent sides (the base angles) are, themselves, congruent and of equal value.

Therefore,

(1)   Let *x* = the measure of each base angle.

(2)   Then *x* + 30 = the measure of the vertex angle.

We can solve for *x* algebraically by keeping in mind that the sum of all the measures will be 180°.

$x + x + (x + 30) = 180$ Simplifying, $3x + 30 = 180$, then $3x = 150$

Therefore, the base angles each measure 50°, and the vertex angle measures 80°.

Quadrilaterals

A **quadrilateral** is a polygon with four sides.

Parallelograms

A **parallelogram** is a quadrilateral whose opposite sides are parallel. Opposite sides of a parallelogram are equal.

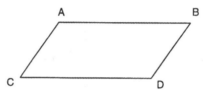

Two angles that have their vertices at the endpoints of the same side of a parallelogram are called **consecutive angles**.

The perpendicular segment connecting any point of a line containing one side of the parallelogram to the line containing the opposite side of the parallelogram is called the **altitude** of the parallelogram.

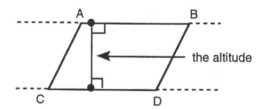

A **diagonal** of a polygon is a line segment joining any two non-consecutive vertices.

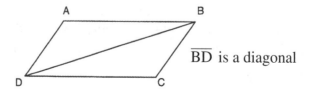

The **area** of a parallelogram is given by the formula $A = bh$, where b is the base and h is the height drawn perpendicular to that base. Note that the height equals the altitude of the parallelogram.

$A = bh$

$A = (10)\,(3)$

$A = 30$

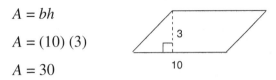

Rectangles

A **rectangle** is a parallelogram with right angles.

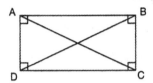

The diagonals of a rectangle are equal.

If the diagonals of a parallelogram are equal, the parallelogram is a rectangle.

If a quadrilateral has four right angles, then it is a rectangle.

The area of a rectangle is given by the formula $A = lw$, where l is the length and w is the width.

$A = lw$

$A = (3)\,(10)$

$A = 30$

Rhombi

A **rhombus** is a parallelogram with two adjacent sides equal.

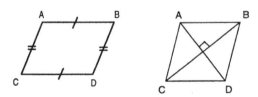

All sides of a rhombus are equal.

The diagonals of a rhombus are perpendicular to each other.

The diagonals of a rhombus bisect the angles of the rhombus.

If the diagonals of a parallelogram are perpendicular, the parallelogram is a rhombus.

If a quadrilateral has four equal sides, then it is a rhombus.

A parallelogram is a rhombus if either diagonal of the parallelogram bisects the angles of the vertices it joins.

Squares

A **square** is a rhombus with a right angle. All 4 angles are necessarily right angles.

A square is an equilateral quadrilateral.

A square has all the properties of parallelograms and rectangles.

A rhombus is a square if one of its interior angles is a right angle.

In a square, the measure of either diagonal can be calculated by multiplying the length of any side by the square root of 2.

The area of a square is given by the formula $A = s^2$, where s is the side of the square. Since all sides of a square are equal, it does not matter which side is used.

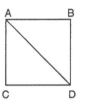

$AD = AB\sqrt{2}$

$A = s^2$

$A = 6^2$

$A = 36$

The area of a square can also be found by taking $\frac{1}{2}$ the product of the length of the diagonal squared.

$A = \frac{1}{2} d^2$

$A = \frac{1}{2} (8)^2$

$A = 32$

Trapezoids

A **trapezoid** is a quadrilateral with two and only two sides parallel. The parallel sides of a trapezoid are called **bases**.

The **median** of a trapezoid is the line segment joining the midpoints of the non-parallel sides.

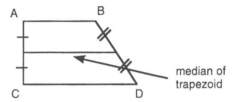

median of trapezoid

The perpendicular segment connecting any point in the line containing one base of the trapezoid to the line containing the other base is the **altitude** of the trapezoid.

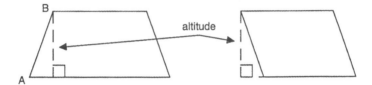

altitude

An **isosceles trapezoid** is a trapezoid whose non-parallel sides are equal. A pair of angles including only one of the parallel sides is called **a pair of base angles**.

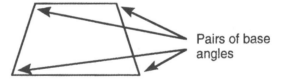

Pairs of base angles

The median of a trapezoid is parallel to the bases and equal to one-half their sum.

The base angles of an isosceles trapezoid are equal. $\angle$ A = $\angle$ B and $\angle$ ADC = $\angle$ BCD

The diagonals of an isosceles trapezoid are equal.

The opposite angles of an isosceles trapezoid are supplementary.

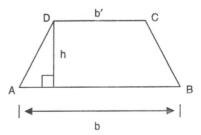

The left angles of a trapezoid are supplementary, as are the right angles, since they are same-side interior angles to parallel lines.

The area of a trapezoid equals one-half the height times the sum of its bases.

Exercise: Quadrilaterals

DIRECTIONS: Refer to the diagram and find the appropriate solution.

Parallelograms, Rectangles, Rhombi, Squares, Trapezoids

1. Find the area of parallelogram *STUV*.

    (A) 56   (B) 90

    (C) 108   (D) 162

    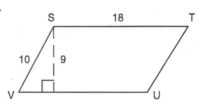

2. If the perimeter of rectangle *PQRS* is 40, find *x*.

    (A) 31   (B) 38

    (C) 2   (D) 44

    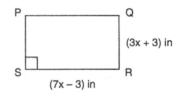

3. In rectangle *ABCD*, *AD* = 6 cm and *DC* = 8 cm. Find the length of the diagonal *AC*.

    (A) 10 cm   (B) 12 cm

    (C) 20 cm   (D) 28 cm

    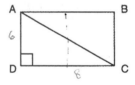

Circles

A **circle** is a set of points in the same plane equidistant from a fixed point called its center.

A **radius** of a circle is a line segment drawn from the center of the circle to any point on the circle.

A portion of a circle is called an **arc** of the circle.

A line that intersects a circle in two points is called a **secant.**

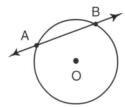

A line segment joining two points on a circle is called a **chord** of the circle.

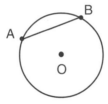

A chord that passes through the center of the circle is called a **diameter** of the circle.

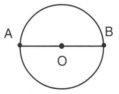

The line passing through the centers of two (or more) circles is called the **line of centers**.

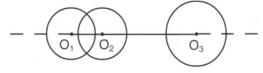

An angle whose vertex is on the circle and whose sides are chords of the circle is called an **inscribed angle**.

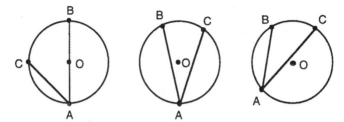

The measure of an inscribed angle is one-half the measure of its intercepted arc $m\angle CAB = \dfrac{1}{2} m\,\widehat{CB}$

An angle whose vertex is at the center of a circle and whose sides are radii is called a **central angle.**

The measure of a **minor arc** is the measure of the central angle that intercepts that arc.

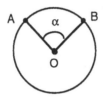

$$m\,\widehat{AB} = \alpha = m\angle AOB$$

The distance from a point P to a given circle is the distance from that point to the point where the circle intersects with a line segment with endpoints at the center of the circle and point P.

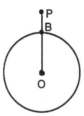

The distance of point P to the diagrammed circle with center O is the line segment PB of line segment PO.

A line that has one and only one point of intersection with a circle is called a tangent to that circle, while their common point is called a **point of tangency**.

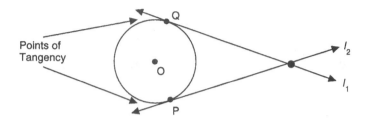

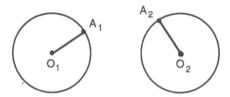

Congruent circles are circles whose radii are congruent.

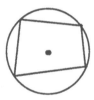

If $O_1A_1 \cong O_2A_2$, then Circle $O_1 \cong$ Circle O_2.

The measure of a semicircle is 180°.

A **circumscribed circle** is a circle passing through all the vertices of a polygon.

Circles that have the same center and unequal radii are called **concentric circles**.

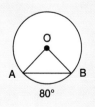

Concentric Circles

PROBLEM

In circle O, the measure of $\overset{\frown}{AB}$ is 80°. Find the measure of $\angle A$.

SOLUTION

The accompanying figure shows that $\overset{\frown}{AB}$ is intercepted by central angle *AOB*. By definition, we know that the measure of the central angle is the measure of its intercepted arc. In this case,

$$m\,\overset{\frown}{AB} = m \angle AOB = 80°$$

Radius *OA* and radius *OB* are congruent and form two sides of Δ *OAB*. By a theorem, the angles opposite these two congruent sides must, themselves, be congruent. Therefore, $m \angle A = m \angle B$.

The sum of the measures of the angles of a triangle is 180°. Therefore,

$$m \angle A + m \angle B + m \angle AOB = 180°$$

Since $m \angle A = m \angle B$, we can write

$$m \angle A + m \angle A + 80° = 180°$$

or $\qquad 2m \angle A = 100°$

or $\qquad m \angle A = 50°$

Therefore, the measure of $\angle A$ is 50°.

PROBLEM

If $m\,\overset{\frown}{BC} = 60°$ and $AB = AC$, what is $m \angle B$?

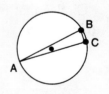

SOLUTION

$$m \angle A = \frac{1}{2} m\,\overset{\frown}{BC} = 30°. \text{ Since } AB = AC, m \angle B = m \angle C. \text{ Let } m \angle B$$
= *x*. Then $x + x + 30° = 180°$. Solving, $x = 75°$.

Exercise: Circles

DIRECTIONS: Simplify the following expressions.

Circumference, Area, Concentric Circles

1. Find the circumference of circle *A* if its radius is 3 mm.

    (A) 3π mm   (B) 6π mm   (C) 9π mm   (D) 12π mm

2. The area of circle *B* is 225π cm². Find the length of the diameter of the circle.

    (A) 15 cm   (B) 20 cm   (C) 30 cm   (D) 20π cm

3. Find the area of the sector shown.

    (A) $\dfrac{9\pi \text{ mm}^2}{4}$ (B) $\dfrac{9\pi \text{ mm}^2}{2}$

    (C) 18 mm²   (D) 6π mm²

Solids

Solid geometry is the study of figures which consist of points not all in the same plane.

Rectangular Solids

A solid with lateral faces and bases that are rectangles is called a **rectangular solid**.

The surface area of a rectangular solid is the sum of the areas of all the faces.

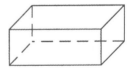

The volume of a rectangular solid is equal to the product of its length, width, and height.

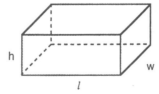

$V = lwh$

PROBLEM

> What are the dimensions of a solid cube whose surface area is numerically equal to its volume?

SOLUTION

The surface area of a cube of edge length a is equal to the sum of the areas of its six faces. Since a cube is a regular polygon, all six faces are congruent. Each face of a cube is a square of edge length a. Hence, the surface area of a cube of edge length a is

$$S = 6a^2$$

The volume of a cube of edge length a is

$$V = a^3$$

We require that $A = V$, or that

$$6a^2 = a^3 \quad \text{or} \quad a = 6$$

Hence, if a cube has edge length 6, its surface area will be numerically equal to its volume.

Cluster II, Macro B

Coordinate Geometry

Coordinate geometry refers to the study of geometric figures using algebraic principles.

The graph shown is called the Cartesian coordinate plane. The graph consists of a pair of perpendicular lines called **coordinate axes**. The **vertical axis** is the y-axis and the **horizontal axis** is the x-axis. The point of intersection of these two axes is called the **origin**; it is the zero point of both axes.

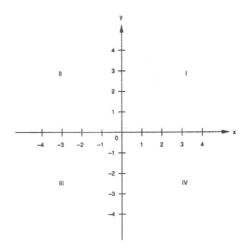

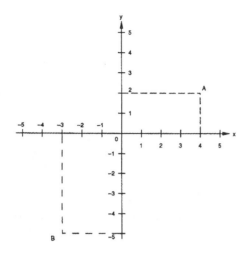

The four regions cut off by the coordinate axes are, in counter-clockwise direction from the top right, called the first, second, third and fourth quadrant, respectively. The first quadrant contains all points with two positive coordinates.

In the graph shown, two points are identified by the ordered pair (x, y) of numbers. The x-coordinate is the first number and the y-coordinate is the second number.

To plot a point on the graph when given the coordinates, draw perpendicular lines from the number-line coordinates to the point where the two lines intersect.

To find the coordinates of a given point on the graph, draw perpendicular lines from the point to the coordinates on the number line. The x-coordinate is written before the y-coordinate and a comma is used to separate the two.

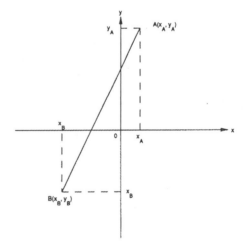

In this case, point A has the coordinates $(4, 2)$ and the coordinates of point B are $(-3, -5)$.

For any two points A and B with coordinates (x_A, y_A) and (x_B, y_B), respectively, the distance between A and B is represented by

$$AB = \sqrt{\left(x_A - x_B\right)^2 + \left(y_A - y_B\right)^2}$$

This is commonly known as the distance formula, a variation of the **Pythagorean Theorem**.

PROBLEM

Find the distance between points $A(1, 3)$ and $B(5, 3)$.

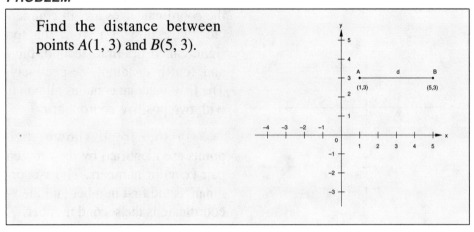

SOLUTION

In this case, where the ordinate of both points is the same, the distance between the two points is given by the absolute value of the difference between the two abscissas. In fact, this case reduces to merely counting boxes as the figure shows.

Let $\quad x_1 = $ abscissa of A $\qquad$ $y_1 = $ ordinate of A

$\qquad\quad x_2 = $ abscissa of B $\qquad$ $y_2 = $ ordinate of B

$\qquad\quad d \ = \ $ the distance

Therefore, $d = |\, x_1 - x_2\, |$. By substitution, $d = |\, 1 - 5\, | = |-4\,| = 4$. This answer can also be obtained by applying the general formula for distance between any two points

$$d = \sqrt{\left(x_1 - x_2\right)^2 + \left(y_1 - y_2\right)^2}$$

By substitution,

$$d = \sqrt{\left(1 - 5\right)^2 + \left(3 - 3\right)^2} = \sqrt{\left(-4\right)^2 + \left(0\right)^2} = \sqrt{16} = 4$$

The distance is 4.

To find the midpoint of a segment between the two given endpoints, use the formula

$$MP = \left(\frac{x_1 + x_2}{2}, \frac{y_1 + y_2}{2}\right)$$

where x_1 and y_1 are the coordinates of one point, and x_2 and y_2 are the coordinates of the other point.

Exercise: Coordinate Geometry

DIRECTIONS: Refer to the diagram and find the appropriate solution.

1. The correct *y*-coordinate for point *R* is what number?

   (A) – 7

   (B) 2

   (C) – 2

   (D) 7

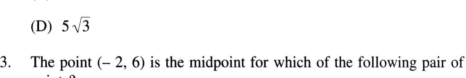

2. How far from the origin is the point (3, 4)?

   (A) 3

   (B) 4

   (C) 5

   (D) $5\sqrt{3}$

3. The point (– 2, 6) is the midpoint for which of the following pair of points?

   (A) (1, 3) and (– 5, 9)   (B) (– 1, – 3) and (5, 9)

   (C) (1, 4) and (5, 9)   (D) (– 1, 4) and (3, – 8)

Transformations

Transformations of plane figures involve changing their appearance and/or location. The four major types of transformations are **rotations, reflections, translations**, and **dilations**.

A **rotation** means turning a figure a specified number of degrees with respect to a fixed point.

Example

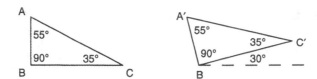

All sizes of the three sides remain the same, but $\overline{BC}$ has been rotated 30° counter-clockwise about the fixed point B. A becomes A′ and C becomes C′.

To **reflect** means to use a line which acts as a mirror, so that each point in the reflection of the figure is the same distance from the reflection line as the original point.

Example

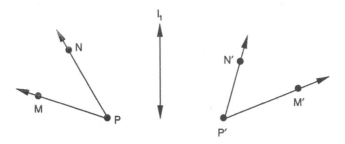

In the above example, the vertical line is the reflection line (denoted l_1). ∠MPN = ∠M′P′N′. Note that M and M′ are equidistant from line l_1. Similarly, for N and N′ and P and P′.

Translation is the act of moving a figure linearly. No change of shape or dimension will occur.

Example

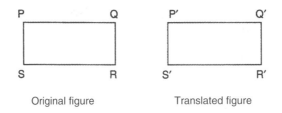

Original figure   Translated figure

Rectangle PQRS has been moved a fixed number of units to the right to produce P′Q′R′S′.

Dilation is the act of changing proportionally the size of a figure, but not its shape.

Example

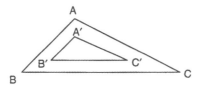

Triangle ABC has been dilated (proportionally reduced) to triangle A'B'C'. Also, ∠A = ∠A', ∠B = ∠B', and ∠C = ∠C'. Dilation can expand as well as reduce.

To **tesselate** a plane means covering it with 2-dimensional figures so that there are no gaps and no two figures overlap.

Example

Covering the floor of a room with non-overlapping square and rectangular tiles.

Cluster II, Macro C

A triangle with one right angle is called a right triangle (below). The side opposite the right angle in a right triangle is called the hypotenuse of the right triangle. The other two sides are called the legs of the right triangle.

A triangle that does not contain a right angle is called an oblique triangle.

The sum of the interior angles of a triangle is 180°.

A triangle can have at most one right or obtuse angle.

If a triangle has two equal angles, then the sides opposite those angles are equal.

If two sides of a triangle are equal, then the angles opposite those sides are equal.

The sum of the exterior angles of a triangle, taking one angle at each vertex, is 360°.

A line that bisects one side of a triangle and is parallel to a second side, bisects the third side.

In a right triangle, the square of the hypotenuse is equal to the sum of the squares of the other two sides (below). This is commonly known as the theorem of Pythagoras or the Pythagorean theorem.

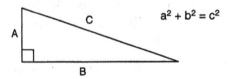

$$a^2 + b^2 = c^2$$

A portion of a circle is called an **arc** of the circle (below).

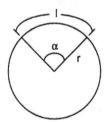

An angle whose vertex is at the center of a circle and whose sides are radii is called a central angle.

If α is the central angle in radians and r is the length of the radius of the circle, then the length of the intercepted arc l is given by $l = \alpha \times r$.

Trigonometric Ratios

Given a right triangle $\triangle ABC$ as shown below:

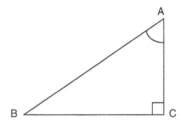

Definition 1: $\sin A = \dfrac{BC}{AB} = \dfrac{\text{measure of side opposite } \angle A}{\text{measure of hypotenuse}}$

Definition 2: $\cos A = \dfrac{AC}{AB} = \dfrac{\text{measure of side adjacent to } \angle A}{\text{measure of hypotenuse}}$

Definition 3: $\tan A = \dfrac{BC}{AC} = \dfrac{\text{measure of side opposite } \angle A}{\text{measure of side adjacent to } \angle A}$

Definition 4: $\cot A = \dfrac{AC}{BC} = \dfrac{\text{measure of side adjacent to } \angle A}{\text{measure of side opposite to } \angle A}$

Definition 5: $\sec A = \dfrac{AB}{AC} = \dfrac{\text{measure of hypotenuse}}{\text{measure of side adjacent to } \angle A}$

Definition 6: $\csc A = \dfrac{AB}{BC} = \dfrac{\text{measure of hypotenuse}}{\text{measure of side opposite } \angle A}$

The following table gives the values of sine, cosine, tangent, and cotangent for some special angles.

α	Sin α	Cos α	Tan α	Cot α
0°	0	1	0	undefined
$\dfrac{\pi}{6}$ rad. = 30°	$\dfrac{1}{2}$	$\dfrac{\sqrt{3}}{2}$	$\dfrac{\sqrt{3}}{3}$	$\sqrt{3}$
$\dfrac{\pi}{4}$ rad. = 45°	$\dfrac{\sqrt{2}}{2}$	$\dfrac{\sqrt{2}}{2}$	1	1
$\dfrac{\pi}{3}$ rad. = 60°	$\dfrac{\sqrt{3}}{2}$	$\dfrac{1}{2}$	$\sqrt{3}$	$\dfrac{\sqrt{3}}{3}$
$\dfrac{\pi}{2}$ rad. = 90°	1	0	undefined	0

PROBLEM

Find tan 635°19′.

SOLUTION

The reference angle of 635°19′ is 2(360°00′) − 635°19′ = −84°41′. Therefore, the tan 635°19′ = 84°41′ = 10.746. (This value may be found from a table of trigonometric functions.) However, the angle 635°19′ is a fourth quadrant angle and the tangent function is negative in the fourth quadrant. Hence, tan 635°19′ = −tan 84°41′ = −10.746.

PROBLEM

Find sin 195°, cos 195°, tan 195°, and cot 195°.

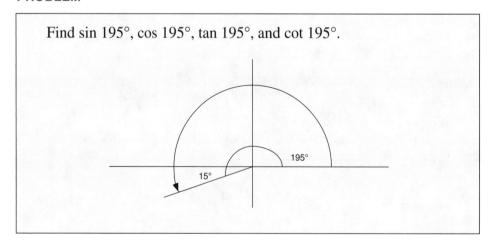

SOLUTION

The reference angle for 195° is 15°. Also, 195° is a third quadrant angle (see figure above).

In the third quadrant, the sine and cosine functions are negative, but the tangent and the cotangent functions are positive. Therefore, sin 195° = –sin 15° = – 0.2588, cos 195° = – cos 15° = – 0.9659, tan 195° = tan 15° = 0.2679, and cot 195° = cot 15° = 3.7321. (Note that the values obtained for the trigonometric functions were found in a table of trigonometric functions.)

Trigonometric Functions

A circle with the center located at the origin of the rectangular coordinate axis and radius equal to one unit length is called a unit circle (below).

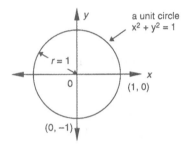

An angle whose vertex is at the origin of a rectangular coordinate system and whose initial side coincides with the positive *x*-axis is said to be in standard position with respect to the coordinate system.

An angle in standard position with respect to a Cartesian coordinate system whose terminal side lies in the first (or second or third or fourth) quadrant is called a first (or second or third or fourth) quadrant angle.

A quadrant angle is an angle in standard position whose terminal side lies on one of the axes of a Cartesian coordinate system.

If θ is a non-quadrantal angle in standard position and $P(x, y)$ is any point, distinct from the origin, on the terminal side of θ (Figures 5.7 and 5.8), then the six trigonometric functions of θ are defined in terms of the abscissa (*x*-coordinate), ordinate (*y*-coordinate), and distance *OP* as follows:

$$\text{sine } \theta = \sin \theta = \frac{\text{ordinate}}{\text{distance}} = \frac{y}{r}$$

$$\text{cosine } \theta = \cos \theta = \frac{\text{abscissa}}{\text{distance}} = \frac{x}{r}$$

$$\text{tangent } \theta = \tan \theta = \frac{\text{ordinate}}{\text{abscissa}} = \frac{y}{x}$$

$$\text{cotangent } \theta = \cot \theta = \frac{\text{abscissa}}{\text{ordinate}} = \frac{x}{y}$$

$$\text{secant } \theta = \sec \theta = \frac{\text{distance}}{\text{abscissa}} = \frac{r}{x}$$

$$\text{cosecant } \theta = \csc \theta = \frac{\text{distance}}{\text{ordinate}} = \frac{r}{y}$$

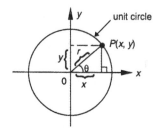 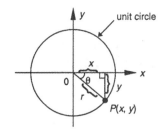

The value of trigonometric functions of quadrantal angles are given in the table below.

θ	$\sin \theta$	$\cos \theta$	$\tan \theta$	$\cot \theta$	$\sec \theta$	$\csc \theta$
0°	0	1	0	∞	1	∞
90°	1	0	∞	0	∞	1
180°	0	−1	0	∞	−1	∞
270°	−1	0	∞	0	∞	−1

The following table gives the signs of all the trigonometric functions for all four quadrants.

Quadrant	$\sin \alpha$	$\cos \alpha$	$\tan \alpha$	$\cot \alpha$	$\sec \alpha$	$\csc \alpha$
I	+	+	+	+	+	+
II	+	−	−	−	−	+
III	−	−	+	+	−	−
IV	−	+	−	−	+	−

NEW JERSEY

HSPA

High School Proficiency Assessment in

Mathematics

CHAPTER 3

Review of Cluster III: Data Analysis, Probability, Statistics, and Discrete Mathematics

Cluster III, Macro A

Probability

Definition of Probability

The probability of an event E is determined by associating 1 with the event occurring (success) and 0 with the event not occurring (failure). The experiment is performed a large number of times.

Independent and Dependent Events: Conditional Probability

An event is a subset of all possible outcomes. Often, instead of saying *event,* we use the term *set.*

Union

The union of two sets, A and B, is the set of all elements that belong to A or to B. The union is denoted by $A \cup B$, read "A or B."

Intersection

The intersection of two sets, A and B, denoted by $A \cap B$, is the set containing all elements that belong to A and to B.

Difference

The difference of two sets, A and B, denoted by $A - B$, is the set of elements in A but not in B.

Complement

The complement of set A, denoted by $\overline{A}$, is the set of elements in the universal set but not in A.

Subset

A is a subset of B, denoted $A \subset B$, if every element of A is an element of B.

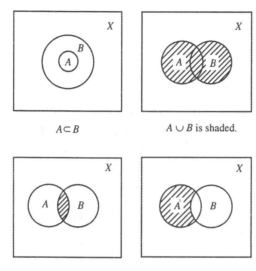

$A \subset B$

$A \cup B$ is shaded.

$A \cap B$ is shaded.

$A - B$ is shaded.

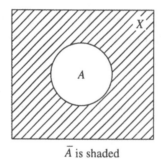

$\overline{A}$ is shaded

We will be frequently using the following identities:

1. $A \cup B = B \cup A$, $A \cap B = B \cap A$

2. $A \cup (B \cup C) = (A \cup B) \cup C$
   $A \cap (B \cap C) = (A \cap B) \cap C$

3. $A \cup (B \cap C) = (A \cup B) \cap (A \cup C)$
   $A \cap (B \cup C) = (A \cap B) \cup (A \cap C)$

4. $\overline{\overline{A}} = A$

5. $A - B = A \cap \overline{B}$

Classical Definition of Probability

Let e denote an event that can happen in k ways out of a total of n ways. All n ways are equally likely. The probability of occurrence of the event e is defined as

$$p = pr\{e\} = \frac{k}{n}$$

The probability of occurrence of e is called its success. The probability of failure (non-occurrence) of the event is denoted by q.

$$q = pr\{\text{not } e\} = \frac{n-k}{n} = 1 - \frac{k}{n} = 1 - p$$

Hence, $p + q = 1$. The event "not e" is denoted by $\tilde{e}$ or $\sim e$.

Example

A toss of a coin will produce one of two possible outcomes: heads or tails. Let e be the event that tails will turn up in a single toss of a coin.

Then

$$p = \frac{1}{1+1} = \frac{1}{2}.$$

Since there is one way a tail can turn up, the numerator is 1; since a single toss can result in a head or a tail, the denominator is 2.

Example

We define the event e to be number 5 or 6 turning up in a single toss of a die. There are six equally likely outcomes of a single toss of a die.

$$\{1, 2, 3, 4, 5, 6\}$$

Thus, $n = 6$. The event e can occur in two ways:

$$p = pr\{e\} = \frac{2}{6} = \frac{1}{3}.$$

Probability of failure of e is

$$q = pr\{\sim e\} = 1 - \frac{1}{3} = \frac{2}{3}.$$

For any event e,

$$0 \leq pr\{e\} \leq 1$$

If the event cannot occur, its probability is 0. If the event must occur, its probability is 1.

Next, we define the odds. Let p be the probability that an event will occur. The odds in favor of its occurrence are $p : q$ and the odds against it are $q : p$.

Example

We determine the probability that at least one tail appears in two tosses of a coin. Let h denote heads and t tails. The possible outcomes of two tosses are

$$(h, h), (h, t), (t, h), (t, t)$$

Three cases are favorable. Thus, $p \text{ (success)} = \dfrac{3}{4}$ and $p \text{ (failure)} = \dfrac{1}{4}$.

The odds in favor of at least one tail are $\dfrac{3}{4} : \dfrac{1}{4} = 3 : 1$.

Example

The event e is that the sum 8 appears in a single toss of a pair of dice. There are $6 \times 6 = 36$ outcomes:

$$(1, 1), (2, 1), (3, 1), \dots , (6, 6).$$

The sum 8 appears in five cases:

$$(2, 6), (6, 2), (3, 5), (5, 3), (4, 4).$$

Then

$$p\{e\} = \frac{5}{36} \quad \text{and} \quad p\{\sim e\} = \frac{31}{36}$$

The odds in favor of a sum of 8 are $\dfrac{5}{36} : \dfrac{31}{36} = 5 : 31$.

The concept of probability is based on the concept of a random experiment. A random experiment is an experiment with more than one possible outcome, conducted in such a way that it is not known in advance which outcome will occur. The set of possible outcomes is denoted by a capital letter, say, X. Usually, each outcome is either a number (a toss of a die) or something to which a number can be assigned (heads = 1, tails = 0, for a toss of a coin).

For some experiments, the number of possible outcomes is infinite.

PROBLEM

> What is the probability of throwing a 6 with a single die?

SOLUTION

The die may land in any of six ways: 1, 2, 3, 4, 5, or 6. The probability of throwing a 6 is,

$$P(6) = \frac{\text{number of ways to get a 6}}{\text{number of ways the die may land}}$$

Thus, $P(6) = \frac{1}{6}$.

PROBLEM

> What is the probability of making a 7 in one throw of a pair of dice?

SOLUTION

There are $6 \times 6 = 36$ ways that two dice can be thrown, as shown below.

1, 1	1, 2	1, 3	1, 4	1, 5	1, 6
2, 1	2, 2	2, 3	2, 4	2, 5	2, 6
3, 1	3, 2	3, 3	3, 4	3, 5	3, 6
4, 1	4, 2	4, 3	4, 4	4, 5	4, 6
5, 1	5, 2	5, 3	5, 4	5, 5	5, 6
6, 1	6, 2	6, 3	6, 4	6, 5	6, 6

The number of possible ways that a 7 will appear are circled. Let us call this set B. Thus,

$$B = \{(1, 6), (2, 5), (3, 4), (4, 3), (5, 2), (6, 1)\}$$

Thus,

$$p(B) = \frac{6}{36} = \frac{1}{6}.$$

Conditional Probability

The probability that E occurs, given that F has occurred, is denoted by

$$P\,(E\mid F)$$

or $P(E$ given $F)$ and is called the conditional probability of E given that F has occurred.

The event that "both E and F occur" is denoted by $E \cap F$ and is called a compound event.

We have

$$P(E|F) = \frac{P(E \cap F)}{P(F)}$$

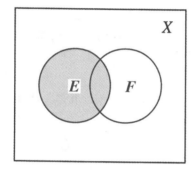   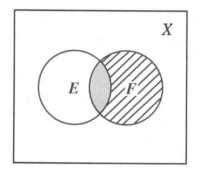

$P(E) =$
$$\frac{\text{shaded}}{\text{shaded} + \text{unshaded}}$$

$P(E|F) =$
$$\frac{\text{shaded}}{\text{shaded} + \text{crosshatched}}$$

Often, we can find the probability of an intersection from

$$P\,(E \cap F) = P\,(E \mid F)\,P\,(F).$$

If

$$P\,(E \mid F) = P\,(E),$$

then we say that events E and F are independent, which means the occurrence of one does not increase or decrease the chances of the other one occurring; otherwise, they are dependent. If E and F are independent, then

$$P\,(E \cap F) = P\,(E) \times P\,(F).$$

For three events, $E,\ F,$ and $G,$ we have

$$P(E \cap F \cap G) = P(E) \ P(F \mid E) P(G \mid E \cap F).$$

If events *E, F,* and *G* are independent, then

$$P(E \cap F \cap G) = P(E) \times P(F) \times P(G).$$

One should not confuse independent events with mutually exclusive events. Two or more events are called mutually exclusive if the occurrence of any one of them excludes the occurrence of the others.

If *E* and *F* are independent, then

$$P(E \mid F) = P(E).$$

If *E* and *F* are mutually exclusive, then

$$P(E|F) = \frac{P(E \cap F)}{P(F)} = \frac{P(\emptyset)}{P(F)} = 0.$$

Let $E_1, E_2, ..., E_n$ be a partition of the set Ω of all outcomes, i.e.,

$$E_i \cap E_j = \emptyset \ \text{for} \ i \neq j \quad (E_i \text{ and } E_j \text{ are mutually exclusive})$$

and

$$\bigcup_{i=1}^{n} E_i = \Omega.$$

Then

$$p(E_1 | E) = \frac{P(E_1)P(E|E_1)}{\sum\limits_{i=1}^{n} P(E_n)P(E|E_n)}$$

This last equation is called Bayes' Theorem.

PROBLEM

There are two roads between towns A and B. There are three roads between towns B and C. How many different routes may one travel between towns A and C?

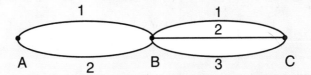

SOLUTION

If we take road 1 from town A to town B and then any road from B to C, there are three ways to travel from A to C. If we take road 2 from A to B and then any road from B to C, there are again three ways to travel from A to C. These two possibilities are the only ones available to us. Thus, there are $3 + 3 = 6$ ways to travel from A to C.

This problem illustrates the fundamental principle of counting. This principle states that if an event can be divided into k components and there are n_1 ways to carry out the first component, n_2 ways to carry out the second, n_i ways to carry out the ith, and n_k ways to carry out the kth, then there are $n_1 \times n_2 \times n_3 \times \ldots \times n_k$ ways for the original event to take place.

PROBLEM

Using only the digits 1, 2, 3, 4, 5, and 6, (a) how many different numbers containing three digits can be formed if any digit may be repeated? (b) How many different numbers are possible if no digit may be repeated?

SOLUTION

(a) There are six choices for each of the three digits of the chosen number. Then, $(6)(6)(6) = 6^3 = 216$ numbers.

(b) There are six choices for the first digit, five choices for the second digit, and four choices for the third digit. Then, $(6)(5)(4) = 120$ numbers.

PROBLEM

An ordinary die is tossed twice. What is the probability of getting a 2 on the first toss and an odd number on the second toss?

SOLUTION

These two events are independent.

Only one of the six sides is 2, so $P(2) = \dfrac{1}{6}$.

Since the only odd numbers are 1, 3, and 5, $P(\text{odd number}) = \dfrac{3}{6} = \dfrac{1}{2}$.

Thus, the final probability $= \left(\dfrac{1}{6}\right)\left(\dfrac{1}{2}\right) = \dfrac{1}{12}$.

PROBLEM

A committee is composed of six Democrats and five Republicans. Three of the Democrats are men, and three of the Republicans are men. If a man is chosen for chairperson, what is the probability that he is a Republican?

$\frac{3}{6} + \frac{3}{5} = \frac{6}{11} = \frac{1}{2}.$

SOLUTION

Let E_1 be the event that a man is chosen, and E_2 the event that the man is a Republican.

We are looking for $P(E_2|E_1)$, From the definition of conditional probability $P(E_2|E_1) = \dfrac{P(E_1 \cap E_2)}{P(E_1)}$.

Of the 11 committee members, three are both male and Republican, hence,

$$P(E_1 \cap E_2) = \frac{\text{number of male Republicans}}{\text{number of committee members}} = \frac{3}{11}.$$

Of all the members, six are men (three Democrats and three Republicans); therefore,

$$P(E_1) = \frac{6}{11}.$$

Furthermore, $\qquad P(E_2|E_1) = \dfrac{P(E_1 \cap E_2)}{P(E_1)} = \dfrac{3/11}{6/11} = \dfrac{3}{6} = \dfrac{1}{2}.$

Experimental Probability

Experimental probability is also known as empirical probability, and is a relative frequency approach that is based on data of past experience.

Example

When 1000 people had been administered a certain drug, 350 of them had an allergic reaction. Then the probability that a new individual will have an allergic reaction to the drug is 350/1000.

Theoretical Probability

Theoretical probability is also known as classical probability, and is based on a sample space of equally likely outcomes. The theoretical probability of any event A is the number of favorable outcomes in A divided by the number of outcomes in the sample space.

Example

An ordinary six-sided die is rolled once. The probability of getting a "2" is 1/6, since there are six outcomes in the sample space, but only one favorable outcome.

Relative Frequency: Large Numbers

The classical definition of probability includes the assumption that all possible outcomes are equally likely. Often, this is not the case. The statistical definition of probability is based on the notion of the relative frequency.

We define the statistical probability or empirical probability of an event as the relative frequency of occurrence of the event when the number of observations is very large. The probability is the limit of the relative frequency as the number of observations increases indefinitely.

Example

Suppose a coin was tossed 1,000 times and the result was 587 tails. The relative frequency of tails is $\dfrac{587}{1000}$. Another 1,000 tosses led to 511 tails.

Then, the combined relative frequency of tails is $\dfrac{1098}{2000}$.

Proceeding in this manner, we obtain a sequence of numbers, which gets closer and closer to the number defined as the probability of a tail in a single toss.

The empirical probability is based on the principle called the Law of Large Numbers.

The Law of Large Numbers

The sample mean (average of the items in our sample) tends to approach the population mean (average of entire population).

Here, by an event, we understand a subset of possible outcomes. It may contain none, one, some, or all of the possible outcomes.

Now we can define probability.

Cluster III, Macro B

Scatter Plot

A **scatter plot** is a graph of ordered pairs of numbers (x,y) where x is the independent variable and y is the dependent variable.

Example

Let x = age in years and y = height in inches. The points (30, 72), (25, 68), and (40, 74) would represent the following three people:

Person 1: 30 years old and 72 inches tall

Person 2: 25 years old and 68 inches tall

Person 3: 40 years old and 74 inches tall

Outlier

An extremely high or low data value when compared to the other data in a set is called an **outlier**.

Example

A sample consists of five numbers: 18, 27, 32, 48, and 4000. The number 4000 is an outlier.

Correlation

A statistical method to determine whether a significant relationship exists among variables is called a **correlation**.

Example

Suppose we know the ages at death of 1000 males and the ages at death of the fathers of each of those males. We would be interested in examining the age at death of each male and the corresponding age at death of his respective father.

Curve Fitting

Curve fitting is also known as the curve of best fit. It involves drawing a curve through or as near to as many parts of the scatter plot as possible.

Probability Distributions

Discrete Distributions

Variable X can assume a discrete set of values x_1, x_2, ..., x_n with probabilities $p_1, p_2, ..., p_n$, respectively, where

$$p_1 + p_2 + ... + p_n = 1.$$

This defines a discrete probability distribution for X.

Probability function, or frequency function, is defined by

$$p : x_i \rightarrow p_i \quad i = 1,2,...,n$$
$$p(x_i) = p_i.$$

Variable X, which assumes certain values with given probabilities, is called a discrete random variable.

Example

A pair of dice is tossed. X denotes the sum of the points obtained, $X = 2$, 3, ..., 12. The probability distribution is given by

x	2	3	4	5	6	7	8	9	10	11	12
$p(x)$	$\frac{1}{36}$	$\frac{2}{36}$	$\frac{3}{36}$	$\frac{4}{36}$	$\frac{5}{36}$	$\frac{6}{36}$	$\frac{5}{36}$	$\frac{4}{36}$	$\frac{3}{36}$	$\frac{2}{36}$	$\frac{1}{36}$

$$\sum p(x) = 1$$

Replacing probabilities with relative frequencies, we obtain from the probability distribution a relative frequency distribution. Probability distributions are for populations, while relative frequency distributions are for samples drawn from this population.

The probability distribution, like a relative frequency distribution, can be represented graphically.

Cumulative probability distributions are obtained by cumulating probabilities.

Example

Find the probability of boys and girls in families with four children. Probabilities for boys and girls are equal.

B = event "boy"

G = event "girl"

$$P(B) = P(G) = \frac{1}{2}$$

1. Four boys

$$P(B \cap B \cap B \cap B) = P(B) \times P(B) \times P(B) \times P(B) = \frac{1}{16}$$

2. Three boys and one girl

$$P[(B \cap B \cap B \cap G) \cup (B \cap B \cap G \cap B)$$
$$\cup (B \cap G \cap B \cap B) \cup (G \cap B \cap B \cap B)]$$
$$= P(B) \times P(B) \times P(B) \times P(G) \times 4$$
$$= \frac{1}{2} \times \frac{1}{2} \times \frac{1}{2} \times \frac{1}{2} \times 4 = \frac{1}{4}$$

3. Three girls and one boy is the same as above

$$p = \frac{1}{4}$$

4. Two boys and two girls

$$P[(B \cap B \cap G \cap G) \cup (B \cap G \cap B \cap G) \cup (B \cap G \cap G \cap B)$$
$$\cup (G \cap G \cap B \cap B) \cup (G \cap B \cap G \cap B) \cup (G \cap B \cap B \cap G)]$$
$$= P(B) \times P(B) \times P(G) \times P(G) \times 6 = \frac{6}{16} = \frac{3}{8}$$

5. Four girls

$$p = \frac{1}{16}$$

Number of Girls x	4	3	2	1	0
Probability $p(X)$	$\dfrac{1}{16}$	$\dfrac{4}{16}$	$\dfrac{6}{16}$	$\dfrac{4}{16}$	$\dfrac{1}{16}$

Here, X is a random variable showing the number of girls in families with four children. The probability distribution is shown in the table.

This distribution can be represented graphically.

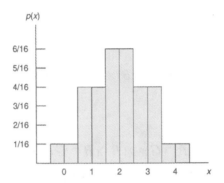

The sum of the areas of the rectangles is 1. Here, the discrete variable X is treated as a continuous variable. The figure is called a probability histogram.

Continuous Distributions

Suppose variable X can assume a continuous set of values. In such a case, the relative frequency polygon of a sample becomes (or rather tends to) a continuous curve.

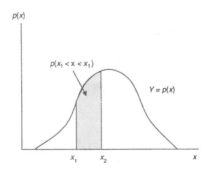

The total area under this curve is 1. The shaded area between the lines $x = x_1$ and $x = x_2$ is equal to the probability that x lies between x_1 and x_2.

Function $p(x)$ is a probability density function. Such a function defines a continuous probability distribution for X. The variable X is called a continuous random variable.

PROBLEM

Suppose the earnings of a laborer, denoted by X, are given by the following probability function.

X	0	8	12	16
$Pr(X = x)$	0.3	0.2	0.3	0.2

Find the laborer's expected earnings.

SOLUTION

The laborer's expected earnings are denoted by $E(X)$, the expected value of the random variable X.

The expected value of X is defined to be

$E(X) = (0)\ Pr(X = 0) + (8)\ Pr(X = 8)$

$+ (12)\ Pr(X = 12) + (16)\ Pr(X = 16)$

$= (0)(.3) + (8)(.2) + (12)(.3) + (16)(.2)$

$= 0 + 1.6 + 3.6 + 3.2 = 8.4$

Thus, the expected earnings are 8.4.

Cluster III, Macro C

Data Interpretation

Some of the problems test ability to apply information given in graphs and tables.

PROBLEM

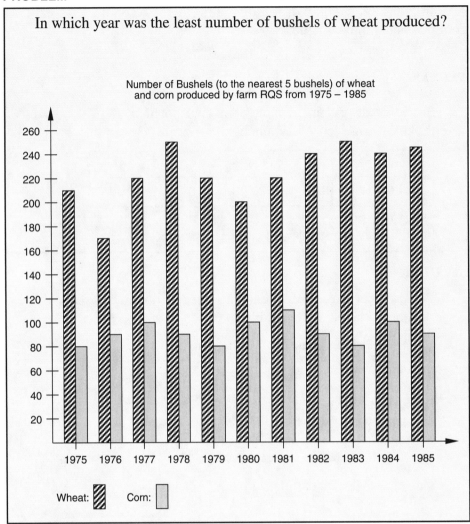

In which year was the least number of bushels of wheat produced?

Number of Bushels (to the nearest 5 bushels) of wheat
and corn produced by farm RQS from 1975 – 1985

Wheat: ▧   Corn: ▢

SOLUTION

By inspection of the graph, we find that the shortest bar representing wheat production is the one representing the wheat production for 1976. Thus, the least number of bushels of wheat was produced in 1976.

PROBLEM

What was the ratio of wheat production in 1985 to that of 1975?

SOLUTION

From the graph representing wheat production, the number of bushels of wheat produced in 1975 is equal to 210 bushels. This number can be found by locating the bar on the graph representing wheat production in 1975 and then drawing a horizontal line from the top of that bar to the vertical axis. The point where this horizontal line meets the vertical axis represents the number of bushels of wheat produced in 1975. This number on the vertical axis is 210. Similarly, the graph indicates that the number of bushels of wheat produced in 1985 is equal to 245 bushels.

Thus, the ratio of wheat production in 1985 to that of 1975 is 245 to 210, which can be written as $^{245}/_{210}$. Simplifying this ratio to its simplest form yields

$$\frac{245}{210} = \frac{5 \times 7 \times 7}{2 \times 3 \times 5 \times 7} = \frac{7}{2 \times 3} = \frac{7}{6} \text{ or } 7:6$$

Answers as Measures of Central Tendency

Usually, averages are called measures of central tendency. We will be using different kinds of averages, such as the arithmetic mean, the geometric mean, and the harmonic mean. A different average should be applied depending on the data, the purpose, and the required accuracy.

Notation and Definitions of Means

By $x_1, x_2, ..., x_n$

we denote the measurements observed in a sample of size n. The letter i in x_i is called a subscript or index. It stands for any of the numbers $1, 2, ..., n$.

Throughout this section, we will be using the summation notation. The symbol

$$\sum_{i=1}^{n} x_i$$

denotes the sum of all x_i's, that is,

$$\sum_{i=1}^{n} x_i = x_1 + x_2 + ... + x_{n-1} + x_n$$

Example

$$\sum_{i=1}^{4} x_i y_i = x_1 y_1 + x_2 y_2 + x_3 y_3 + x_4 y_4$$

Example

Let a be a constant. Then

$$\sum_{k=1}^{n} ax_k = ax_1 + ax_2 + \ldots + ax_n$$

$$= a(x_1 + x_2 + \ldots + x_n)$$

$$= a\sum_{k=1}^{n} x_k$$

In general,

$$\sum ax_k = a\sum x_k$$

and, if a and b are both constants,

$$\sum (ax + by) = a\sum x + b\sum y$$

Often, when no confusion can arise, we write $\sum_{k} x_k$ instead of $\sum_{k=1}^{n} x_k$.

Definition of Arithmetic Mean

The arithmetic mean, or mean, of a set of measurements is the sum of the measurements divided by the total number of measurements.

The arithmetic mean of a set of numbers $x_1, x_2, \ldots, x_n$ is denoted by $\bar{x}$ (read "x bar").

$$\bar{x} = \frac{\sum_{i=1}^{n} x_1}{n} = \frac{x_1 + x_2 + \ldots + x_n}{n}$$

Example

The arithmetic mean of the numbers 3, 7, 1, 24, 11, and 32 is

$$\bar{x} = \frac{3+7+1+24+11+32}{6} = 13$$

Example

Let $f_1, f_2, \ldots, f_n$ be the frequencies of the numbers $x_1, x_2, \ldots, x_n$ (i.e., number x_i occurs f_i times). The arithmetic mean is

$$\bar{x} = \frac{f_1 x_1 + f_2 x_2 + \ldots + f_n x_n}{f_1 + f_2 + \ldots + f_n} = \frac{\sum\limits_{i=1}^{n} f_i x_i}{\sum\limits_{i=1}^{n} f_i}$$

$$= \frac{\sum fx}{\sum f}.$$

Note that the total frequency, that is, the total number of cases, is

$$\sum_{i=1}^{n} f_i.$$

Example

If the measurements 3, 7, 2, 8, 0, and 4 occur with frequencies 3, 2, 1, 5, 10, and 6, respectively, then the arithmetic mean is

$$\bar{x} = \frac{3 \times 3 + 7 \times 2 + 2 \times 1 + 8 \times 5 + 0 \times 10 + 4 \times 6}{3 + 2 + 1 + 5 + 10 + 6} \approx 3.3$$

Keep in mind that the arithmetic mean is strongly affected by extreme values.

Example

Consider four workers whose monthly salaries are $2,500, $3,200, $3,700, and $48,000. The arithmetic mean of their salaries is

$$\frac{\$57,400}{4} = \$14,350$$

The figure $14,350 can hardly represent the typical monthly salary of the four workers.

Example

The deviation d_i of x_i from its mean x is defined to be

$$d_i = x_i - \bar{x}$$

The sum of the deviations of $x_1, x_2, \ldots, x_n$ from their mean x is equal to zero. Indeed,

$$\sum_{i=1}^{n} d_i = \sum_{i=1}^{n} (x_i - \bar{x}) = 0$$

Thus,

$$\sum_{i=1}^{n} (x_i - \bar{x}) = \sum_{i=1}^{n} x_i - n\bar{x} = \sum x_i - n \frac{\sum x_i}{n}$$

$$= \sum x_i - \sum x_i = 0.$$

Example

If $z_1 = x_1 + y_1, \ldots, z_n = x_n + y_n$, then $\bar{z} = \bar{x} + \bar{y}$. Indeed,

$$\bar{x} = \frac{\sum x}{n}, \bar{y} = \frac{\sum y}{n}, \text{ and } \bar{z} = \frac{\sum z}{n}.$$

We have

$$\bar{z} = \frac{\sum z}{n} = \frac{\sum (x+y)}{n} = \frac{\sum x}{n} + \frac{\sum y}{n} = \bar{x} + \bar{y}.$$

The arithmetic mean plays an important role in statistical inference.

We will be using different symbols for the sample mean and the population mean. The population mean is denoted by μ, and the sample mean is denoted by $\bar{x}$. The sample mean $\bar{x}$ will be used to make inferences about the corresponding population mean μ.

Example

Suppose a bank has 500 savings accounts. We pick a sample of 12 accounts. The balance on each account in dollars is

657	284	51
215	73	327
65	412	218
539	225	195

The sample mean $\bar{x}$ is

$$\bar{x} = \frac{\sum_{i=1}^{12} x_i}{12} = \$271.75$$

The average amount of money for the 12 sampled accounts is $271.75. Using this information, we estimate the total amount of money in the bank attributable to savings accounts to be

$$\$271.75 \times 500 = \$135,875.$$

PROBLEM

> The following measurements were taken by an antique dealer as he weighed to the nearest pound his prized collection of anvils. The weights were 84, 92, 37, 50, 50, 84, 40, and 98 pounds. What was the mean weight of the anvils?

SOLUTION

The average or mean weight of the anvils is

$$\bar{x} = \frac{\text{sum of observations}}{\text{number of observations}}$$

$$= \frac{84 + 92 + 37 + 50 + 50 + 84 + 40 + 98}{8}$$

$$= \frac{535}{8} = 66.88 \cong 67 \text{ pounds}$$

An alternate way to compute the sample mean is to rearrange the terms in the numerator, grouping the numbers that are the same. Thus,

$$\bar{x} = \frac{(84 + 84) + (50 + 50) + 37 + 40 + 92 + 98}{8}$$

We see that we can express the mean in terms of the frequency of observations. The frequency of an observation is the number of times a number appears in a sample.

$$\bar{x} = \frac{2(84) + 2(50) + 37 + 40 + 92 + 98}{8}$$

The observations 84 and 50 appear in the sample twice, and thus each observation has frequency 2.

PROBLEM

> The numbers 4, 2, 7, and 9 occur with frequencies 2, 3, 11, and 4, respectively. Find the arithmetic mean.

SOLUTION

To find the arithmetic mean, $\bar{x}$, multiply each different number by its associated frequency. Add these products, then divide by the total number of numbers.

$$\bar{x} = [(4)(2) + (2)(3) + (7)(11) + (9)(4)] \div 20$$
$$= (8 + 6 + 77 + 36) \div 20$$
$$= 127 \div 20 = 6.35$$

PROBLEM

> A student takes two quizzes, one midterm, and one final exam in a statistics course. The midterm counts three times as much as a quiz, and the final exam counts five times as much as a quiz. If the quiz scores were 70 and 80, the midterm score was 65, and the final exam score was 85, what was the weighted average?

SOLUTION

$$x = [(70)(1) + (80)(1) + (65)(3) + (85)(5)] \div 10$$
$$= (70 + 80 + 195 + 425) \div 10$$
$$= 770 \div 10 = 77$$

Example

During four successive years, the prices of gasoline were 70, 75, 78, and 95 cents per gallon. Find the average cost of gasoline over the four-year period. There are two methods of computing this average.

Method 1

Suppose the car owner used 100 gallons each year. Then

$$\text{Average Cost} = \frac{\text{total cost}}{\text{total number of gallons}}$$

$$= \frac{0.7 \times 100 + 0.75 \times 100 + 0.78 \times 100 + 0.95 \times 100}{400}$$

$$= \$0.795 \ / \ \text{gal}$$

Method 2

Suppose the car owner spends $100 on gasoline each year. Then

$$\text{Average Cost} = \frac{\text{total cost}}{\text{total number of gallons}}$$

$$= \$\frac{400}{509.66} = 0.785 \ / \ \text{gal}$$

509.66 is the result of 100/0.70 + 100/0.75 + 100/0.78 + 100/0.95. Each fraction represents the number of gallons of gas bought in a single year, depending on the price per gallon.

Both averages are correct. Depending on assumed conditions, we obtain different answers.

Suggestion:

Let x_1, x_2, ... x_n be a set of numbers, g = geometric mean, and h = harmonic mean. Then $g = \sqrt[n]{(x_1)(x_2)(...)(x_n)}$, i.e.: the nth root of the product of the numbers.

$$h = \frac{n}{\left(\dfrac{1}{x_1} + \dfrac{1}{x_2} + ... + \dfrac{1}{x_n}\right)},$$

i.e., the reciprocal of the arithmetic mean of the reciprocal of each number. To justify $h \le g \le \bar{x}$, let $x_1 = 2$, $x_2 = 3$, $x_3 = 5$, $x_4 = 10$

$$\bar{x} = \frac{2+3+5+10}{4} = 5$$

$$g = \sqrt[4]{(2)(3)(5)(10)} = \sqrt[4]{300} \approx 4.16$$

$$h = \frac{4}{\left(\dfrac{1}{2} + \dfrac{1}{3} + \dfrac{1}{5} + \dfrac{1}{10}\right)} = \frac{4}{1.1\overline{3}} \approx 3.53$$

so $h \le g \le \bar{x}$.

Let g be the geometric mean of a set of positive numbers $x_1, x_2, \ldots, x_n$, and let $\bar{x}$ be the arithmetic mean and h the harmonic mean. Then

$$h \leq g \leq \bar{x}$$

The equality holds only if all the numbers $x_1, x_2, \ldots, x_n$ are identical.

PROBLEM

A motor car traveled 3 consecutive miles, the first mile at $x_1 = 35$ miles per hour (mph), the second at $x_2 = 48$ mph, and the third at $x_3 = 40$ mph. Find the average speed of the car in miles per hour.

SOLUTION

Distance = Rate × Time. Therefore, Time = $\dfrac{\text{Distance}}{\text{Rate}}$.

For the first mile, Time = $\dfrac{1 \text{ mile}}{35 \text{ miles/hour}} = \dfrac{1}{35}$ hour.

For the second mile, Time = $\dfrac{1 \text{ mile}}{48 \text{ miles/hour}} = \dfrac{1}{48}$ hour.

For the third mile, Time = $\dfrac{1 \text{ mile}}{40 \text{ miles/hour}} = \dfrac{1}{40}$ hour.

Total time = $T_1 + T_2 + T_3 = \dfrac{1}{35} + \dfrac{1}{48} + \dfrac{1}{40}$.

Converting to decimals, $\text{Time}_{tot} = .0287 + .0208 + .025$

$$= .0745 \text{ hours.}$$

The average speed can be computed by the following formula:

Average Speed $= \dfrac{\text{Total distance}}{\text{Total time}} = \dfrac{3 \text{ miles}}{.0745 \text{ hours}} = 40.32$ mph.

Average speed is an example of a harmonic mean. The harmonic mean is

$$h = \dfrac{3}{\dfrac{1}{T_1} + \dfrac{1}{T_2} + \dfrac{1}{T_3}}.$$

Measures of Central Tendency

Definition of the Mode

The mode of a set of numbers is that value which occurs most often (with the highest frequency).

Observe that the mode may not exist. Also, if the mode exists, it may not be unique. For example, for the numbers 1, 1, 2, and 2, the mode is not unique.

Example

The set of numbers 2, 2, 4, 7, 9, 9, 13, 13, 13, 26, and 29 has mode 13.

The set of numbers that has two modes is called **bimodal.**

Example

The set 3, 4, 4, 4, 5, 6, 6, 6, 7, 7 is bimodal, with modes of 4 and 6.

For grouped data – data presented in the form of a frequency table – we do not know the actual measurements, only how many measurements fall into each interval. In such a case, the mode is the midpoint of the class interval with the highest frequency.

Note that the mode can also measure popularity. In this sense, we can determine the most popular model of car or the most popular actor.

Example

One can compute the mode from a histogram or frequency distribution.

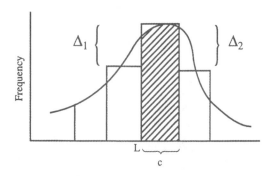

The shaded area indicates the modal class, that is, the class containing the mode.

Since the model class is 15–19, the mode equals $\dfrac{15+19}{2}=17$

Class	Frequency
10–14	2
15–19	5
20–20	1

$$Mode = L + c\left[\frac{\Delta_1}{\Delta_1 + \Delta_2}\right]$$

where L is the lower class boundary of the modal class

c is the size of the modal class interval

Δ_1 is the excess of the modal frequency over the frequency of the next lower class

Δ_2 is the excess of the modal frequency over the frequency of the next higher class

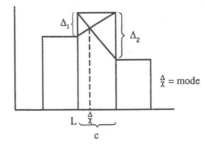

PROBLEM

Find the mode of the sample 14, 19, 16, 21, 18, 19, 24, 15, and 19.

SOLUTION

The mode is another measure of central tendency in a data set. It is the observation or observations that occur with the greatest frequency. The number 19 is observed three times in this sample, and no other observation appears as frequently. The mode of this sample is therefore 19.

PROBLEM

Find the mode or modes of the sample 6, 7, 7, 3, 8, 5, 3, and 9.

SOLUTION

In this sample the numbers 7 and 3 both appear twice. There are no other observations that appear as frequently as these two. Therefore, 3 and 7 are the modes of this sample. The sample is called "bimodal."

PROBLEM

Find the mode of the sample 14, 16, 21, 19, 18, 24, and 17.

SOLUTION

In this sample all the numbers occur with the same frequency. There is no single number that is observed more frequently than any other. Thus, there is no mode or all observations are modes. The mode is not a useful concept here.

Definition of Median

The median of a set of numbers is defined as the middle value when the numbers are arranged in order of magnitude.

Usually, the median is used to measure the midpoint of a large set of numbers. For example, we can talk about the median age of people getting married. Here, the median reflects the central value of the data for a large set of measurements. For small sets of numbers, we use the following conventions:

— For an odd number of measurements, the median is the middle value.

— For an even number of measurements, the median is the average of the two middle values.

In both cases, the numbers have to be arranged in order of magnitude.

Example

The scores of a test are 78, 79, 83, 83, 87, 92, and 95. Hence, the median is 83.

Example

The median of the set of numbers 21, 25, 29, 33, 44, and 47 is $\frac{29+33}{2} = 31$.

It is more difficult to compute the median for grouped data. The exact value of the measurements is not known; hence, we know only that the median is located in a particular class interval. The problem is where to place the median within this interval.

For grouped data, the median obtained by interpolation is given by

$$\text{Median} = L + \frac{c}{f_{\text{median}}}\left(\frac{n}{2} - \left(\sum f\right)\right)^{\text{cum}}$$

where L = the lower class limit of the interval that contains the median

c = the size of the median class interval

f_{median} = the frequency of the median class

n = the total frequency

$(\Sigma f)_{\text{cum}}$ = the sum of frequencies (cumulative frequency) for all classes before the median class

PROBLEM

Find the median of the sample 34, 29, 26, 37, and 31.

SOLUTION

The median, a measure of central tendency, is the middle number. The number of observations that lie above the median is the same as the number of observations that lie below it.

Arranged in order we have 26, 29, 31, 34, and 37. The number of observations is odd, and thus the median is 31. Note that there are two numbers in the sample above 31 and two below 31.

PROBLEM

Find the median of the sample 34, 29, 26, 37, 31, and 34.

SOLUTION

The sample arranged in order is 26, 29, 31, 34, 34, and 37. The number of observations is even and thus the median, or middle number, is chosen halfway between the third and fourth numbers. In this case, the median is

$$\frac{31+34}{2} = 32.5$$

Example

The weight of 50 men is depicted in the table below in the form of frequency distribution.

Weight	Frequency
115 – 121	2
122 – 128	3
129 – 135	13
136 – 142	15
143 – 149	9
150 – 156	5
157 – 163	3
Total	50

Class 136 – 142 has the highest frequency.

The mode is the midpoint of the class interval with the highest frequency.

$$\text{Mode} = \frac{135.5 + 142.5}{2} = 139$$

The median is located in class 136 – 142.

We have

$$\text{Median} = L + \frac{c}{f_{\text{median}}} \left[\frac{n}{2} - \left[\sum f \right]_{\text{cum}} \right]$$

where

$$L = 135.5$$

$$c = 7$$

$$f_{\text{median}} = 15$$

$$n = 50$$

$$(\Sigma f)_{\text{cum}} = 2 + 3 + 13 = 18$$

Hence,

$$\text{Median} = 135.5 + \frac{7}{15}\left[\frac{50}{2} - 18\right] = 138.77$$

To compute the arithmetic mean for grouped data, we compute midpoint x_i of each of the intervals and use the formula

$$\bar{x} = \frac{\displaystyle\sum_{i=1}^{n} f_i x_i}{\displaystyle\sum_{i=1}^{n} f_i}$$

We have

$$\bar{x} = \frac{118 \times 2 + 125 \times 3 + 132 \times 13 + 139 \times 15 + 146 \times 9 + 153 \times 5 + 160 \times 3}{50}$$

$$= 139.42.$$

For symmetrical curves, the mean, mode, and median all coincide.

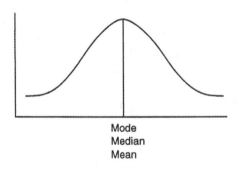

Mode
Median
Mean

For skewed distributions, we have the following.

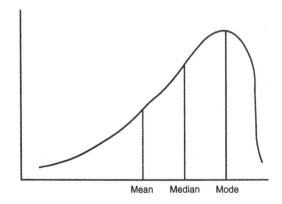

Mean   Median   Mode

The distribution is skewed to the left.

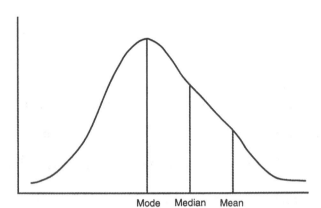

The distribution is skewed to the right.

Class Boundaries	Class Midpoints	Frequencies
58.5 – 61.5	60	4
61.5 – 64.5	63	8
64.5 – 67.5	66	12
67.5 – 70.5	69	13
70.5 – 73.5	72	21
73.5 – 76.5	75	15
76.5 – 79.5	78	12
79.5 – 82.5	81	9
82.5 – 85.5	84	4
85.5 – 88.5	87	2

PROBLEM

Find the median weight from the previous table.

SOLUTION

There are 100 observations in the sample. The median will be the 50th observation. When using an even-numbered sample of grouped data, the convention is to call the $\frac{n}{2}$th observation the median. There are 37 observations in the first four intervals, and the first five intervals contain 58 observations. The 50th observation is in the fifth class interval.

We use the technique of linear interpolation to estimate the position of the 50th observation within the class interval.

The width of the fifth class is three, and there are 21 observations in the class. To interpolate we imagine that each observation takes up $\frac{3}{21}$ units of the interval. There are 37 observations in the first four intervals, and thus the 13th observation in the fifth class will be the median.

This 13th observation will be approximately $13\left(\frac{3}{21}\right)$ units from the lower boundary of the fifth class interval. The median is thus the lower boundary of the fifth class plus $13\left(\frac{3}{21}\right)$ or

$$\text{median} = 70.5 + \frac{13}{7} = 72.36.$$

PROBLEM

A sample of drivers involved in motor vehicle accidents was categorized by age. The results appear as:

Age	Number of Accidents
16 – 25	28
26 – 35	13
36 – 45	12
46 – 55	8
56 – 65	19
66 – 75	20

What is the value of the median?

SOLUTION

We seek the $\frac{100}{2} = 50$th number, which appears in the third class (36 – 45).

The total number of accidents is 100. The median is the $\frac{100}{2} = 50$th number when the numbers are arranged in ascending order. (In this case, we have intervals of numbers instead of just numbers.) The two intervals $16 - 25$ and $26 - 35$ consist of 41 count. We need nine numbers from the interval $36 -$ 45. Use the lower boundary of this interval $36 - 45$, which is 35.5, and add $\frac{9}{12}$ of the width of the interval (10, which equals $45.5 - 35.5$). Then

$$35.5 + \frac{9}{12} (10) = 43$$

Cluster III, Macro D

Counting & Sorting Techniques

Counting and sorting techniques are a systematic way of identifying the number of ways possible in a mathematical setting.

Example

At a certain company, a 3-character security code consists of 2 different letters, followed by an odd digit. To find the number of different security codes, we multiply 26 by 25 by 5 = (26)(25)(5) = 3250. The logic for this is: there are any one of 26 letters for the first character, but only 25 letters available for the second character, since no repetition is allowed. Finally, only the digits 1, 3, 5, 7, and 9 may be used for the third character.

Trees:

A **tree** is a graphical device used to illustrate a sequence of events.

Example

A person travels from Philadelphia to Pittsburgh to Los Angeles. From Philadelphia to Pittsburgh, he will travel by auto, train, or bus. From Pittsburgh to Los Angeles, he will go by train or plane. Let A=Philadelphia, B=Pittsburgh, and C=Los Angeles. The following is an appropriate tree diagram representing all possible modes of travel.

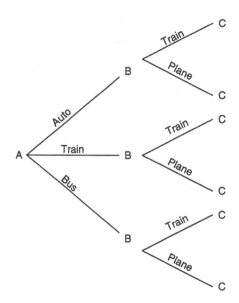

Networks:

A **network** is a diagram of vertices and connecting paths.

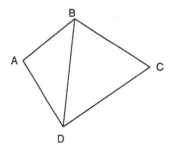

Example

Let A, B, C, and D represent 4 cities, where line segments represent connecting flights. Thus, while cities B and D have a connecting flight, there is no direct flight between cities A and C.

Combinational Analysis

If an event can happen in any one of *n* ways, and if, when this has occurred, another event can happen in any one of *m* ways, then the number of ways in which both events can happen in the specified order is

$$n \times m.$$

Example

A bank offers three types of checking accounts and four types of savings accounts. Any customer who wants to have both accounts has $3 \times 4 = 12$ possibilities.

Example

In how many ways can six children be arranged in a row?

Each of six children can fill the first position. Then, each of five remaining children can fill the second place. Thus, there are 6×5 ways of filling the first two places. There are four ways of filling the third place, three ways of filling the fourth place, two ways of filling the fifth place, and one way of filling the sixth place. Hence,

Number of arrangements $= 6 \times 5 \times 4 \times 3 \times 2 \times 1 = 6! = 720$

Note: !(factorial) represents the product of all integers from 1 to a given number.

We have a general rule: number of arrangements of n different objects in a row is $n!$.

Permutations

The number of permutations, or arrangements, of n distinct objects taken K at a time, where $k \leq n$, is given by $_nP_k = n(n-1)(n-2)(\ldots)(n-k+1) = \dfrac{n!}{(n-k)!}$.

The order in which objects are taken is important.

Example

The number of permutations of the letters a, b, c, d, e taken 3 at a time is

$$_5P_3 = (5)(4)(3) = 60 = \frac{5!}{(5-3)!}$$

Combinations

The number of ways one can choose k objects out of the n objects, disregarding the order, is denoted by

$$_nC_k, C(n,k) \text{ or } \binom{n}{k}$$

and is equal to

$$_nC_k = \frac{n(n-1)\ldots(n-k+1)}{k!} = \frac{n!}{k!(n-k)!} = \frac{_nP_k}{k!}$$

$_nC_k$ is the number of combinations of n objects taken k at a time.

Example

The number of combinations of the letters x, y, and z, taken two at a time, is

$$_3C_2 = \frac{3!}{2!(3-2)!} = 3$$

The combinations are xy, xz, and yz. Combinations xy and yx are the same, but permutations xy and yx are not the same.

Example

A committee consists of seven people. There are 13 candidates. In how many ways can the committee be chosen?

$$_{13}C_7 = \frac{13!}{7!6!} = \frac{8 \times 9 \times 10 \times 11 \times 12 \times 13}{2 \times 3 \times 4 \times 5 \times 6} = 1,716$$

Example

How many possible outcomes does a lotto game have when a player chooses seven numbers out of 49 numbers?

$$_{49}C_7 = \frac{49!}{7!42!} = \frac{43 \times 44 \times 45 \times 46 \times 47 \times 48 \times 49}{2 \times 3 \times 4 \times 5 \times 6 \times 7}$$
$$= 85,900,584$$

Note: $_nC_k = {_nC_{n-k}}$.

For example, $_{49}C_7 = \frac{49!}{7!42!} = \frac{49!}{42!7!} = {_{49}C_{42}}$

The number of combinations of n objects taken 1, 2, …, n at a time is

$$_nC_1 + {_nC_2} + \ldots + {_nC_n} = 2^n - 1$$

It is difficult to evaluate $n!$ for large numbers. In such cases, an approximate formula (called Stirling's Formula) is used:

$$n! \approx \sqrt{2\pi n}\, n^n e^{-n}$$

where e is the natural base of logarithms, $e = 2.718281828\ldots$

Example

Determine the probability of four 4's in six tosses of a die. The result of each toss is the event 4 or non 4 ($\overline{4}$). Thus,

$$4, 4, 4, \overline{4}, 4, \overline{4}$$

or

$$\overline{4}, 4, 4, \overline{4}, 4, 4$$

are successes.

The probability of an event $4, 4, 4, \overline{4}, 4, \overline{4}$ is

$$P(4, 4, 4, \overline{4}, 4, \overline{4}) = \frac{1}{6} \times \frac{1}{6} \times \frac{1}{6} \times \frac{5}{6} \times \frac{1}{6} \times \frac{5}{6}$$

$$= \left(\frac{1}{6}\right)^4 \times \left(\frac{5}{6}\right)^2$$

All events in which four 4's and two non 4's occur have the same probability. The number of such events is

$$_6C_4 = \frac{6!}{4!2!} = 15$$

and all these events are mutually exclusive. Hence,

$$P(\text{four 4's in 6 tosses}) = 15 \times \left(\frac{1}{6}\right)^4 \times \left(\frac{5}{6}\right)^2 = 0.008$$

Example

Thirty percent of the cars produced by a factory have some defect. A sample of 100 cars is selected at random. What is the probability that

1. exactly 10 cars will be defective?

2. 95 or more will be defective?

In general, if $p = p(E)$ and $q = p(\overline{E})$, then the probability of getting exactly m E's in n trials is

$$_nC_m p^m q^{n-m}$$

1. $p(10 \text{ defective cars}) = {}_{100}C_{10}\left(\dfrac{3}{10}\right)^{10}\left(\dfrac{7}{10}\right)^{90} \approx .00000117$

2. $p(95 \text{ or more defective}) = p(95 \text{ defective}) +$

    $p(96 \text{ defective}) + p(97 \text{ defective}) + p(98 \text{ defective}) +$

    $p(99 \text{ defective}) + p(100 \text{ defective}) =$

    $$= {}_{100}C_{95}\left(\frac{3}{10}\right)^{95}\left(\frac{7}{10}\right)^{5} + {}_{100}C_{96}\left(\frac{3}{10}\right)^{96}\left(\frac{7}{10}\right)^{4}$$

    $$+ \ldots + {}_{100}C_{100}\left(\frac{3}{10}\right)^{100}\left(\frac{7}{10}\right)^{0} \approx 2.74 \times 10^{-43}$$

PROBLEM

> How many baseball teams of nine members can be chosen from among 12 players, without regard to the position played by each member?

SOLUTION

Since there is no regard to position, this is a combinations problem (if order or arrangement had been important, it would have been a permutations problem as well). The general formula for the number of combinations of n things taken r at a time is

$$C(n,r) = \frac{n!}{r!(n-r)!}.$$

We have to find the number of combinations of 12 things taken nine at a time. Hence, we have

$$C(12,9) = \frac{12!}{9!(12-9)!} = \frac{12!}{9!3!} = \frac{12 \times 11 \times 10 \times 9!}{3 \times 2 \times 1 \times 9!} = 220.$$

Therefore, there are 220 possible teams.

PROBLEM

What is the probability of getting exactly four 6's when a die is rolled seven times?

SOLUTION

Let X = the number of 6's observed when a die is rolled seven times. If we assume that each roll is independent of each other roll and that the probability of rolling a 6 on one roll is $= \frac{1}{6}$, the X is binomially distributed with parameters $n = 7$ and $p = \frac{1}{6}$.

Thus, $Pr(X = 4) = Pr$(exactly four 6's on seven rolls)

$$= {}_7C_4 \bullet \left(\frac{1}{6}\right)^4 \left(\frac{5}{6}\right)^{7-4}$$

$$= \frac{7 \times 6 \times 5 \times 4 \times 3 \times 2 \times 1}{4 \times 3 \times 2 \times 3 \times 2 \times 1} \left(\frac{1}{6}\right)^4 \left(\frac{5}{6}\right)^3$$

$$= 35 \left(\frac{1}{6}\right)^4 \left(\frac{5}{6}\right)^3$$

$$Pr(X = 4) = 35 \left(\frac{1}{1,296}\right)\left(\frac{125}{216}\right) = \frac{4,375}{279,936} = .0156.$$

Cluster III, Macro E

Iteration & Recursion

The terms **iteration and recursion** refer to a pattern or formula in finding the next term in a graphical description or in a specific numeric sequence.

Example

. . . could represent a pattern of squares whereby the side of each successive square is one-half the side of its predecessor.

Example

2, 6, 18, 54... represents a geometric sequence where each term is three times its predecessor.

Fractals

Fractals are geometric figures which consist of a design repeated infinitely on a decreasing scale.

Example

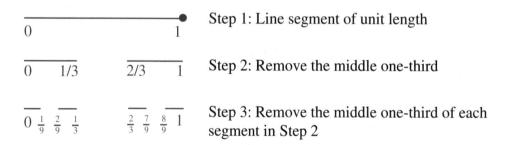

This process can repeat indefinitely.

Algorithms & Flow Charts

Algorithms and flow charts are graphical descriptions of decisions and specific rules to follow.

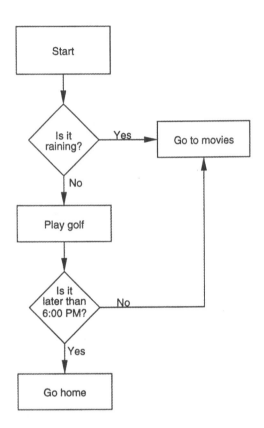

Example

In the above example, a person will go the movies if it is raining. If it is not raining, he will play golf. After playing golf, he will check the time. If it is later than 6:00 PM, he will go home. Otherwise, he will go to the movies.

NEW JERSEY

HSPA

High School Proficiency Assessment in

Mathematics

CHAPTER 4

Review of Cluster IV:
Patterns, Functions, and Algebra

Cluster IV, Macro A

Sequences

A set of numbers u_1, u_2, u_3, ... in a definite order of arrangement and formed according to a definite rule is called a **sequence**. Each number in the sequence is called a term of the sequence. If the number of terms is finite, it is called a finite sequence; otherwise, it is called an infinite sequence.

A general term n can be obtained by applying a general law of formation, by which any term in the sequence can be obtained.

An arithmetic progression (AP) is a sequence of numbers in which each term, excluding the first, is obtained from the preceding one by adding a fixed quantity to it. This constant amount is called the common difference.

Let
a = first term of progression

a_n = nth term of progression

l = last term

d = common difference

k = number of terms

S_n = sum of first n terms, $n \le k$

then
$l = a + (k - 1)d$

$$S_n = \frac{n}{2}(a + a_n) = \frac{n}{2}[2a + (n - 1)d].$$

In general, to find the common difference in a given arithmetic progression, simply subtract any term from its successor.

A single term between two given terms a and b is called the arithmetic mean, M, between these two terms and is given by:

$$M = \frac{a + b}{2}.$$

PROBLEM

> Insert four arithmetic means between 1 and 36.

SOLUTION

The terms between any two given terms of a progression are called the means between these two terms. Inserting four arithmetic means between 1 and 36 requires an arithmetic progression (A.P.) of the form 1, ___, ___, ___, ___, 36, where the second term is the mean of the first and third terms, the third term is the mean of the second and fourth terms, etc. Using the formula, $l = a + (k - 1)d$, for the nth term, we can determine d. Knowing the common difference, d, we can obtain the means by adding d to each preceding number after the first.

$$a = 1, l = 36, \text{ and } k = 6 \text{ since there will be six terms}$$

$$l = a + (k - 1)d$$

$$36 = 1 + 5d$$

$$5d = 35$$

$$d = 7$$

The arithmetic means are: $1 + 7$, $(1 + 7) + 7$, $(1 + 7 + 7) + 7$, $(1 + 7 + 7 + 7) + 7$; that is, 8, 15, 22, and 29. The arithmetic progression is 1, 8, 15, 22, 29, 36.

A **geometric progression** (GP) is a sequence of numbers each of which, after the first, is obtained by multiplying the preceding number by a constant number called the common ratio, r.

Let $a = $ first term

$a_n = n$th term of progression

$r = $ common ratio

$k = $ number of terms

$l = $ last term

$S_n = $ sum of first n terms

then

$$l = ar^{k-1}$$

$$S_n = \frac{a(r^k - 1)}{r - 1} = \frac{rl - a}{r - 1}.$$

The sum to infinity (S_∞) of any geometric progression is

$$S_\infty = \frac{a}{1 - r} \quad \text{if } |r| < 1.$$

To find the common ratio in a given geometric progression, divide any term by its predecessor.

A single term between two given terms of a geometric progression is called the geometric mean between the two terms. The geometric mean is denoted by G.

If G is the geometric mean between the terms a and b, then $\dfrac{a}{G} = \dfrac{G}{b}$ which implies:

$$G^2 = ab \quad \text{or} \quad G = \pm\sqrt{ab}.$$

A **harmonic progression** (HP) is a sequence of numbers whose reciprocals are an arithmetic progression. The terms between any two given terms of a harmonic progression are called the harmonic means between these two terms.

Let $\qquad a = $ first term

$\qquad\qquad a_n = n$th term of progression

$\qquad\qquad l = $ last term

$\qquad\qquad k = $ number of terms

$\qquad\qquad d = $ common difference of the reciprocals

then $\qquad\qquad\qquad a = \dfrac{1}{a_1}, \quad l = \dfrac{1}{l + (k-1)d}.$

PROBLEM

> If a^2, b^2, and c^2 are in arithmetic progression, show that $b + c$, $c + a$, and $a + b$ are in harmonic progression.

SOLUTION

We are given that a^2, b^2, and c^2 are in arithmetic progression. By this we mean that each new term is obtained by adding a constant to the preceding term.

By adding $(ab + ac + bc)$ to each term, we see that

$$a^2 + (ab + ac + bc),\ b^2 + (ab + ac + bc),\ c^2 + (ab + ac + bc)$$

are also in arithmetic progression. These three terms can be rewritten as

$$a^2 + ab + ac + bc,\ b^2 + bc + ab + ac,\ c^2 + ac + bc + ab.$$

Notice that:

$$a^2 + ab + ac + bc = (a + b)(a + c)$$

$$b^2 + bc + ab + ac = (b + c)(b + a)$$

$$c^2 + ac + bc + ab = (c + a)(c + b)$$

Therefore, the three terms can be rewritten as:

$$(a + b)(a + c), (b + c)(b + a), (c + a)(c + b)$$

which are also in arithmetic progression.

Now, dividing each term by $(a + b)(b + c)(c + a)$, we obtain:

$$\frac{1}{b+c}, \quad \frac{1}{c+a}, \quad \frac{1}{a+b}$$

which are in arithmetic progression.

Recall that a sequence of numbers whose reciprocals form an arithmetic progression is called a harmonic progression. Thus, since $\frac{1}{b+c}, \frac{1}{c+a}, \frac{1}{a+b}$ is an arithmetic progression, $b + c$, $c + a$, and $a + b$ are in harmonic progression.

PROBLEM

If the first term of a geometric progression is 9 and the common ratio is $-\frac{2}{3}$, find the first five terms.

SOLUTION

A geometric progression (GP) is a sequence of numbers each of which, after the first, is obtained by multiplying the preceding number by a constant number called the common ratio, r. Thus, a GP such as $a_1, a_2, a_3, a_4, a_5, \ldots$ or $a_1, a_1r, a_2r^2, a_3r^3, a_4r^4, \ldots$ with $a_1 = 9$ and $r = -\frac{2}{3}$ is determined as follows:

$$a_1 = 9$$

$$a_2 = 9\left(-\frac{2}{3}\right) = -6$$

$$a_3 = (-6)\left(-\frac{2}{3}\right) = 4$$

$$a_4 = 4\left(-\frac{2}{3}\right) = -\frac{8}{3}$$

$$a_5 = \left(-\frac{8}{3}\right)\left(-\frac{2}{3}\right) = \frac{16}{9}$$

Thus, the first five terms are: $9, -6, 4, -\frac{8}{3}, \frac{16}{9}$.

PROBLEM

Find the sum of the first ten terms of the geometric progression: 15, 30, 60, 120, …

SOLUTION

A geometric progression is a sequence in which each term after the first is formed by multiplying the preceding term by a fixed number, called the common ratio.

If a is the first term, r is the common ratio, and n is the number of terms, the geometric progression is

$$a, ar, ar^2, …, ar^{n-1}$$

The given GP, 15, 30, 60, 120, …, may be written as 15, 15(2), 15(2^2), 15(2^3) … . The sum, S_n, of the first n terms of the geometric progression is given by

$$S_n = \frac{a(r^n - 1)}{r - 1} \qquad \text{where } a = \text{first term}$$
$$r = \text{common ratio}$$
$$n = \text{number of terms.}$$

Here $a = 15$, $r = 2$, and $n = 10$.

$$S_{10} = \frac{15(2^{10} - 1)}{2 - 1}$$
$$= \frac{15(1{,}024 - 1)}{1}$$
$$= 15(1{,}023)$$
$$= 15{,}345$$

Series

A series is defined as the sum of the terms of a sequence $u_1 + u_2 + u_3 + \ldots + u_n \ldots$

The terms u_1, u_2, u_3, $\ldots$, u_n are called the first, second, third, and nth terms of the series. If the series has a finite number of terms, it is called a finite series, otherwise, it is called an infinite series.

Finite series

$$\sum_{i=1}^{n} u_i = u_1 + u_2 + u_3 + \ldots + u_n$$

Infinite series

$$\sum_{i=1}^{\infty} u_i = u_1 + u_2 + u_3 + \ldots$$

The general, or nth, term of a series is an expression which indicates the law of formation of the terms.

PROBLEM

Determine the general term of the series:

$$\frac{1}{5} + \frac{3}{125} + \frac{5}{3125} + \frac{7}{78,125} + \ldots$$

SOLUTION

The numerators of the terms in the series are consecutive odd numbers beginning with 1. An odd number can be represented by $2n - 1$.

In the denominators, the base is always 5, and the power is a consecutive odd integer beginning with 1.

The general term can therefore be expressed by

$$\frac{2n-1}{5^{2n-1}}, \text{ the series by } \sum_{i=1}^{\infty} \frac{2i-1}{5^{2i-1}}$$

and the series is generated by replacing i with $i = 1, 2, 3, 4, \ldots$.

Let $s_n = u_1 + u_2 + \ldots + u_n$ be the sum of the first n terms of the infinite series $u_1 + u_2 + u_3 + \ldots$. The terms of the sequence $s_1, s_2, s_3 \ldots$ are called the partial sums of the series.

If the values of s_1, s_2, ..., s_n never become greater than or equal to a certain value S—no matter how big n is—and approach S as n increases, the sums are said to have a limit. This is represented by:

$$\lim_{n \to \infty} s_n = S.$$

If $\lim_{n \to \infty} s_n = S$ is a finite number, the series $u_1 + u_2 + u_3 + ...$ is convergent and S is called the sum of the infinite series.

A series which is not convergent is said to be divergent.

An alternating series is one whose terms are alternately positive and negative. An alternating series converges if:

A) After a certain number of terms the absolute value of a certain term is less than that of the preceding term.

B) The nth term has a limit of zero as n approaches ∞.

A series is said to be absolutely convergent if the series formed by taking absolute values of the terms converges. A convergent series which is not absolutely convergent is conditionally convergent.

The terms of an absolutely convergent series may be arranged in any order and not affect the convergence.

A series of the form $c_0 + c_1 x + c_2 x^2 + ...$ where the coefficients $c_0, c_1, c_2, ...$ are constants is called a power series in x. It is denoted by

$$\sum_{n=0}^{\infty} c_n x^n.$$

The set of values of x for which a power series converges is called its interval of convergence.

A series of the type $\dfrac{1}{1^p} + \dfrac{1}{2^p} + \dfrac{1}{3^p} + ...$ where p is a constant is known as a p series and is denoted by

$$\sum_{n=1}^{\infty} \frac{1}{n^p}.$$

The p series converges if $p > 1$.

The following methods are used to test convergence of series:

A) Comparison test for convergence of series of positive terms.

If each term of a given series of positive terms is less than or equal to the corresponding term of a known convergent series, then the given series converges.

If each term of a given series of positive terms is greater than or equal to the corresponding term of a known divergent series, then the given series diverges.

PROBLEM

Establish the convergence or divergence of the series:

$$\frac{1}{1+\sqrt{1}} + \frac{1}{1+\sqrt{2}} + \frac{1}{1+\sqrt{3}} + \frac{1}{1+\sqrt{4}} + \dots$$

SOLUTION

To establish the convergence or divergence of the given series, we first determine the nth term of the series. By studying the law of formation of the terms of the series, we find the nth term to be $\frac{1}{1+\sqrt{n}}$.

To determine whether this series is convergent or divergent, we use the comparison test. We choose $\frac{1}{n}$, which is a known divergent series since it is a p-series, $\frac{1}{n^p}$, with $p = 1$. If we can show $\frac{1}{1+\sqrt{n}} > \frac{1}{n}$, then $\frac{1}{1+\sqrt{n}}$ is divergent. But we can see this is true, since $1 + \sqrt{n} < n$ for $n > 2$. Therefore, the given series is divergent.

B) Ratio test:

For a given series $s_1 + s_2 + s_3 + \dots$, it is possible to conclude it is:

Convergent if: $\lim\limits_{n \to \infty} \left| \frac{s_{n+1}}{s_n} \right| = L < 1$

Divergent if: $\lim\limits_{n \to \infty} \left| \frac{s_{n+1}}{s_n} \right| = L > 1$

If $\lim\limits_{n \to \infty} \left| \dfrac{s_{n+1}}{s_n} \right| = L = 1$, the ratio test is not decisive; it fails to establish

convergence or divergence.

PROBLEM

> Find the numerical value of the following:
>
> a) $\displaystyle\sum_{j=1}^{7}(2j+1)$ b) $\displaystyle\sum_{j=1}^{21}(3j-2)$

SOLUTION

If $A(r)$ is some mathematical expression and n is a positive integer, then the symbol $\displaystyle\sum_{r=0}^{n} A(r)$ means "Successively replace" the letter r in the expression $A(r)$ with the numbers $0, 1, 2, \ldots, n$ and add up the terms. The symbol Σ is the Greek letter sigma and is a shorthand way to denote "the sum." It avoids having to write the sum $A(0) + A(1) + A(2) + \ldots + A(n)$.

A) $\displaystyle\sum_{j=1}^{7}(2j+1) = \sum_{j=1}^{7}2j + \sum_{j=1}^{7}1$

$= 2\displaystyle\sum_{j=1}^{7}j + 7$ and since $\displaystyle\sum_{j=1}^{n}j = \frac{n}{2}(1+n)$

we get $2\left(\dfrac{7}{2}\right)(1+7) + 7 = 63$

B) $\displaystyle\sum_{j=1}^{21}(3j-2) = \sum_{j=1}^{21}3j - \sum_{j=1}^{21}2$

$= 3\displaystyle\sum_{j=1}^{21}j - (21)(2) = 3\left(\dfrac{21}{2}\right)(1+21) - (21)(2)$

$= 651$

PROBLEM

> Determine the general term of the sequence:
>
> $$\frac{1}{2},\ \frac{1}{12},\ \frac{1}{30},\ \frac{1}{56},\ \frac{1}{90},\ \ldots$$

SOLUTION

To determine the general term, it is necessary to find how the adjacent terms differ. In this example, it is sufficient to consider the denominator because the numerator is the same for all the terms.

Now we try to write an expression that generates the series. By inspection, each term is the product of two successive integers, for example:

$$\frac{1}{2} = \frac{1}{1} \times \frac{1}{2}, \quad \frac{1}{12} = \frac{1}{3} \times \frac{1}{4}, \quad \frac{1}{30} = \frac{1}{5} \times \frac{1}{6}, \quad \frac{1}{56} = \frac{1}{7} \times \frac{1}{8}$$

This fact can be expressed as

$$\frac{1}{(2n-1)(2n)}$$

and this is the desired answer.

Cluster IV, Macro B

Relations and Functions

A **relation** is any set of ordered pairs. The set of all first members of the ordered pairs is called the **domain** of the relation and the set of all second members of the ordered pairs is called the **range** of the relation.

PROBLEM

> Find the relation defined by $y^2 = 25 - x^2$ where the domain $D = \{0, 3, 4, 5\}$.

SOLUTION

x takes on the values 0, 3, 4, and 5. Replacing x by these values in the equation $y^2 = 25 - x^2$, we obtain the corresponding values of y (see table). Hence the relation defined by $y^2 = 25 - x^2$ where x belongs to $D = \{0, 3, 4, 5\}$ is

$\{(0, 5), (0, -5), (3, 4), (3, -4), (4, 3), (4, -3), (5, 0)\}.$

The domain of the relation is (0, 3, 4, 5). The range of the relation is (5, -5, 4, -4, 3, -3, 0).

A function with domain X and range Y could be given by the table:

x	$y^2 = 25 - x^2$	y
0	$y^2 = 25 - 0$ $y^2 = 25$ $y = \pm\sqrt{25}$ $y = \pm 5$	± 5
3	$y^2 = 25 - 3^2$ $y^2 = 25 - 9$ $y^2 = 16$ $y = \pm\sqrt{16}$ $y = \pm 4$	± 4
4	$y^2 = 25 - 4^2$ $y^2 = 25 - 16$ $y^2 = 9$ $y = \pm\sqrt{9}$ $y = \pm 3$	± 3
5	$y^2 = 25 - 5^2$ $y^2 = 25 - 25$ $y^2 = 0$ $y = 0$	0

A function is a relation in which no two ordered pairs have the same first member. For example: given

$X = \{1, 2, 3, 4, 5, 6, 7, 8\}$ and $Y = \{2, 4, 6, 8\}$

$\{(1, 2), (2, 2), (3, 4), (4, 4), (5, 6), (6, 6), (7, 8), (8, 8)\}$

is a function.

You can see above that every member of the domain is paired with one and only one member of the range. Then this relation is called a function and is represented by $y = f(x)$, where $x \in X$ and $y \in Y$ ($\in$ represents "is an element of.") If f is a function that takes an element $x \in X$ and sends it to an element $y \in Y$, f is said to map x into y. We write this as $f: x \rightarrow y$. For this reason, a function is also called a mapping.

Given $f{:}x \rightarrow y$, we can also say that y is a function of x, denoted $f(x) = y$, "f of x equals y." In this function, y is called the dependent variable, since it derives its value from x. By the same reasoning, x is called the independent variable.

Another way of checking if a relation is a function is the vertical line test: if there does not exist any vertical line which crosses the graph of a relation in more than one place, then the relation is a function. If the domain of a relation or a function is not specified, it is assumed to be all real numbers.

PROBLEM

Find the domain D and the range R of the function $\left(x, \dfrac{x}{|x|} \right)$.

SOLUTION

Note that the y-value of any coordinate pair (x, y) is $\dfrac{x}{|x|}$. We can replace x in the formula $\dfrac{x}{|x|}$ with any number except 0, since the denominator, $|x|$, cannot equal 0 (i.e., $|x| \neq 0$). This is because division by 0 is undefined. Therefore, the domain D is the set of all real numbers except 0. If x is negative, i.e., $x < 0$, then $|x| = -x$ by definition. Hence, if x is negative, then $\dfrac{x}{|x|} = \dfrac{x}{-x} = -1$. If x is positive, i.e. $x > 0$, then $|x| = x$ by definition. Hence, if x is positive, then $\dfrac{x}{|x|} = \dfrac{x}{x} = 1$. (The case where $x = 0$ has already been found to be undefined.) Thus, there are only two numbers -1 and 1 in the range R of the function; that is, $R = \{-1, 1\}$.

PROBLEM

Find the set of ordered pairs $\{(x, y)\}$ if $y = x^2 - 2x - 3$ and $D = \{x \mid x$ is an integer and $1 \leq x \leq 4\}$.

SOLUTION

We first note that $D = \{1, 2, 3, 4\}$. Substituting these values of x in the equation

$$y = x^2 - 2x - 3,$$

we find the corresponding y values. Thus,

for $x = 1$, $y = 1^2 - 2(1) - 3 = 1 - 2 - 3 = -4$

for $x = 2$, $y = 2^2 - 2(2) - 3 = 4 - 4 - 3 = -3$

for $x = 3$, $y = 3^2 - 2(3) - 3 = 9 - 6 - 3 = 0$

for $x = 4$, $y = 4^2 - 2(4) - 3 = 16 - 8 - 3 = 5$

Hence, $\{(x, y)\} = \{(1, -4), (2, -3), (3, 0), (4, 5)\}$.

Properties of Relations

A relation R from set A to set B is a subset of the Cartesian Product $A \times B$ written aRb with $a \in A$ and $b \in B$.

Let R be a relation from a set S to itself. Then

A) R is said to be reflexive if and only if sRs for every $s \in S$.

B) R is said to be symmetric if $s_iRs_j \Rightarrow s_jRs_i$ where $s_i, s_j \in S$.

C) R is said to be transitive if s_iRs_j and s_jRs_k implies s_iRs_k.

D) R is said to be antisymmetric if s_1Rs_2 and s_2Rs_1 implies $s_1 = s_2$.

A relation R on $S \times S$ is called an equivalence relation if R is reflexive, symmetric, and transitive.

Properties of Functions

If f and g are two functions with a common domain, then the sum of f and g, written $f + g$, is defined by:

$$(f + g)(x) = f(x) + g(x)$$

The difference of f and g is defined by:

$$(f - g)(x) = f(x) - g(x)$$

The product of f and g is defined by:

$$fg(x) = f(x)g(x)$$

The quotient of f and g is defined by:

$$\left(\frac{f}{g}\right)(x) = \frac{f(x)}{g(x)}, \text{ where } g(x) \neq 0$$

Example

Let $f(x) = 2x^2$ with domain $D_f = R$ and $g(x) = x - 5$ with $D_g = R$. Find A) $f + g$, B) $f - g$, C) fg, and D) $\frac{f}{g}$.

A) $f + g$ has domain R and

$$(f + g)(x) = f(x) + g(x) = 2x^2 + x - 5$$

for each number x. For example, $(f + g)(1) = f(1) + g(1) = 2(1)^2 + 1 - 5 = 2 - 4 = -2$.

B) $f - g$ has domain R and

$$(f - g)(x) = f(x) - g(x) = 2x^2 - (x - 5) = 2x^2 - x + 5$$

for each number x. For example, $(f - g)(1) = f(1) - g(1) = 2(1)^2 - 1 + 5 = 2 + 4 = 6$.

C) fg has domain R and

$$(fg)(x) = f(x) \bullet g(x) = 2x^2 \bullet (x - 5) = 2x^3 - 10x^2$$

for each number x. In particular, $(fg)(1) = 2(1)^3 - 10(1)^2 = 2 - 10 = -8$.

D) $\frac{f}{g}$ has domain R excluding the number $x = 5$ (when $x = 5$, $g(x) = 0$ and division by zero is undefined) and

$$\left(\frac{f}{g}\right)(x) = \frac{f(x)}{g(x)} = \frac{2x^2}{x - 5}$$

for each number $x \neq 5$. In particular, $\left(\frac{f}{g}\right)(1) = \frac{2(1)^2}{1 - 5} = \frac{2}{-4} = -\frac{1}{2}$.

If f is a function, then the inverse of f, written f^{-1} is such that:

$$(x, y) \in f \Leftrightarrow \text{(implies) } (y, x) \in f^{-1}$$

The graph of f^{-1} can be obtained from the graph of f by simply reflecting the graph of f across the line $y = x$. The graphs of f and f^{-1} are symmetrical about the line $y = x$.

The inverse of a function is not necessarily a function.

PROBLEM

> Show that the inverse of the function $y = x^2 + 4x - 5$ is not a function.

SOLUTION

Given the function f such that no two of its ordered pairs have the same first element, the inverse function f^{-1} is the set of ordered pairs obtained from f by interchanging in each ordered pair the first and second elements. Thus, the inverse of the function

$$y = x^2 + 4x - 5 \text{ is } x = y^2 + 4y - 5.$$

The given function has more than one first component corresponding to a given second component. For example, if $x = 0$, then $y = -5$ or 1. If the elements $(-5, 0)$ and $(1, 0)$ are reversed, we have $(0, -5)$ and $(0, 1)$ as elements of the inverse. Since the first component 0 has more than one second component, the inverse is not a function (a function can have only one y value corresponding to each x value).

A function $f : A \rightarrow B$ is said to be one-to-one or injective if distinct elements in the domain A have distinct images, i.e. if $f(x) = f(y)$ implies $x = y$. For an example: $y = f(x) = x^3$ defined over the domain $\{x \in R \mid x \geq 0\}$ is an injection or an injective function.

A function $f : A \rightarrow B$ is said to be a surjective or an onto function if each element of B is the image of some element of A, i.e., $f(A) = B$. For instance, $y = x \sin x$ is a surjection or a surjective function.

A function $f : A \rightarrow B$ is said to be bijective or a bijection if f is both injective and surjective. f is also called a one-to-one, onto correspondence between A and B. An example of such function would be $y = x$.

PROBLEM

> If $f(x) = x^2 - x - 3$, $g(x) = (x^2 - 1)/(x + 2)$, and $h(x) = f(x) + g(x)$, find $h(2)$.

SOLUTION

$h(x) = f(x) + g(x)$, and we are told that $f(x) = x^2 - x - 3$ and $g(x) = (x^2 - 1)/(x + 2)$; thus, $h(x) = (x^2 - x - 3) + (x^2 - 1)/(x + 2)$.

To find $h(2)$, we replace x by 2 in the above formula for $h(x)$,

$$h(2) = [(2)^2 - 2 - 3] + \left(\frac{2^2 - 1}{2 + 2} \right)$$

$$= (4 - 2 - 3) + \left(\frac{4 - 1}{4} \right)$$

$$= (-1) + \left(\frac{3}{4} \right)$$

$$= -\frac{4}{4} + \frac{3}{4}$$

$$= -\frac{1}{4}$$

Thus, $h(2) = -\frac{1}{4}$.

Cluster IV, Macro C

Linear Equations

An **equation** is defined as a statement that two separate expressions are equal.

A **solution** to the equation is a number that makes the equation true when it is substituted for the variable. For example, in the equation $3x = 18$, 6 is the solution since $3(6) = 18$. Depending on the equation, there can be more than one solution. Equations with the same solutions are said to be **equivalent equations**. An equation without a solution is said to have a solution set that is the **empty** or **null** set and is represented by Ø.

A linear equation in one variable is one that can be put into a form such as $ax + b = 0$, where a and b are constants and $a \neq 0$.

To solve a linear equation means to transform it to the form $x = \frac{-b}{a}$.

A) If the equation has unknowns on both sides of the equality, it is convenient to put similar terms on the same side.

Example

$$4x + 3 = 2x + 9$$
$$4x + 3 - 2x = 2x + 9 - 2x$$
$$(4x - 2x) + 3 = (2x - 2x) + 9$$
$$2x + 3 = 0 + 9$$

$$2x + 3 - 3 = 0 + 9 - 3$$
$$2x = 6$$
$$\frac{2x}{2} = \frac{6}{2}$$
$$x = 3$$

Replacing an expression within an equation by an equivalent expression will result in a new equation with solutions equivalent to the original equation. Consider the equation below:

$$3x + y + x + 2y = 15$$

The left side of the equation can be simplified as follows:

$$3x + y + x + 2y = 4x + 3y$$

Equating the simplified left side to the original right side gives:

$$4x + 3y = 15$$

Performing the same operation on both sides of an equation will result in a new equation that is equivalent to the original equation, as in:

B) **Addition or subtraction**

$$y + 6 = 10$$

We can add $(- 6)$ to both sides

$$y + 6 + (- 6) = 10 + (- 6)$$

to get $y + 0 = 10 - 6$

or, $y = 4$.

C) **Multiplication or division**

$$3x = 6$$
$$\frac{3x}{3} = \frac{6}{3}$$
$$x = 2$$

D) **Raising to a power**

$$a = x^2y$$
$$a^2 = (x^2y)^2$$
$$a^2 = x^4y^2$$

This can be applied to negative and fractional powers as well. For example,

$$x^2 = 3y^4$$

If we raise both members to the -2 power, we get

$$(x^2)^{-2} = (3y^4)^{-2}$$

$$\frac{1}{(x^2)^2} = \frac{1}{(3y^4)^2}$$

$$\frac{1}{x^4} = \frac{1}{9y^8}$$

If we raise both members to the $\frac{1}{2}$ power, which is the same as taking the square root, we get

$$(x^2)^{1/2} = (3y^4)^{1/2}$$

$$x = \sqrt{3}y^2$$

E) If there are radicals in the equation, it is necessary to square both sides and then apply A).

$$\sqrt{3x+1} = 5$$

$$\left(\sqrt{3x+1}\right)^2 = 5^2$$

$$3x + 1 = 25$$

$$3x + 1 - 1 = 25 - 1$$

$$3x = 24$$

$$x = \frac{24}{3}$$

$$x = 8$$

F) If the equation appears in fractional form, it is necessary to transform it using cross-multiplication, and then repeating the same procedure as in A), we obtain:

$$\frac{3x+4}{3} = \frac{7x+2}{5}$$

By using cross-multiplication we would obtain

$$3(7x + 2) = 5(3x + 4)$$

This is equivalent to

$$21x + 6 = 15x + 20$$

which can be solved as in A). Solution: $x = \frac{7}{3}$

G) The **reciprocal** of both members of an equation are equivalent to the original equation. Note: The reciprocal of zero is undefined.

If $\quad \dfrac{2x+y}{z} = \dfrac{5}{2}, \quad$ then $\quad \dfrac{z}{2x+y} = \dfrac{2}{5}$

PROBLEM

> Solve the equation $2(x + 3) = (3x + 5) - (x - 5)$.

SOLUTION

We transform the given equation to an equivalent equation where we can easily recognize the solution set.

$$2(x + 3) \quad = \quad 3x + 5 - (x - 5)$$

Distribute,

$$2x + 6 \quad = \quad 3x + 5 - x + 5$$

Combine terms,

$$2x + 6 \quad = \quad 2x + 10$$

Subtract $2x$ from both sides,

$$6 \quad = \quad 10$$

Since $6 = 10$ is not a true statement, there is no real number which will make the original equation true. The equation is inconsistent and the solution set is $\emptyset$, the empty set.

Exercise: Linear Equations

> **DIRECTIONS**: Solve for the unknown.

1. $\dfrac{1}{3}b + 3 = \dfrac{1}{2}b$

    (A) $\dfrac{1}{2}$ (B) 2   (C) $3\dfrac{3}{5}$ (D) 18

2. $0.4p + 1 = 0.7p - 2$

   (A) 12   (B) 2   (C) 5   (D) 10

3. $4(3x + 2) - 11 = 3(3x - 2)$

   (A) – 3   (B) – 1   (C) 2   (D) 3

Linear Equations in Two Variables

Equations of the form $ax + by = c$, where a, b, and c are constants and $a, b \neq 0$ are called linear equations in two variables. This equation is also known as the general form of a linear equation.

The solution set for a linear equation in two variables is the set of all x and y values for which the equation is true. An element in the solution set is called an ordered pair (x, y) where x and y are two of the values that together satisfy the equation. The x value is always first and is called the x-coordinate. The y value is always second and is called the y-coordinate.

Graphing the Solution Set

The solution set of the equation $ax + by = c$ can be represented by graphing the ordered pairs that satisfy the equation on a rectangular coordinate system. This is a system where two real number lines are drawn at right angles to each other. The x-axis is the horizontal line and the y-axis is the vertical line. The point where the two lines intersect is called the origin and is associated with the ordered pair $(0, 0)$.

To plot a certain ordered pair (x, y), move x units along the x-axis in the direction indicated by the sign of x, and then move y units along the y-axis in the direction indicated by the sign of y. Note that movement to the right or up is positive, while movement to the left or down is negative.

Example

Graph the following points: $(1, 2)$, $(-3, 2)$, $(-2, -1)$, $(1, -1)$. (See figure below.)

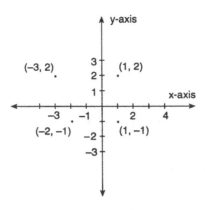

To graph a linear equation in two variables, it is necessary to graph its solution set; that is, draw a line through the points whose coordinates satisfy the equation. The resultant graph of a linear equation in two variables is a straight line.

There are several ways of graphing the line $ax + by = c$ (see figure below), and two of them are shown below:

A)   Plot two or more ordered pairs that satisfy the equation and then draw the straight line through these points.

B)   Plot the points $A\left(\dfrac{c}{a}, 0\right)$ and $B\left(0, \dfrac{c}{b}\right)$ that correspond to the points

where the line intersects the *x*-axis and *y*-axis, respectively, as shown:

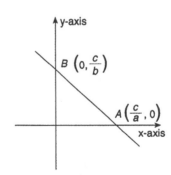

The slope of the line containing two points (x_1, y_1) and (x_2, y_2) is given by:

$$\text{Slope} = m = \frac{y_2 - y_1}{x_2 - x_1}$$

Horizontal lines have a slope of zero, and the slope of vertical lines is undefined. Parallel lines have equal slopes and perpendicular lines have slopes that are negative reciprocals of each other.

The equation of a line with slope m passing through a point $Q(x_0, y_0)$ is of the form:

$$y - y_0 = m(x - x_0)$$

This is called the *point-slope form* of a linear equation.

The equation of a line passing through $Q(x_1, y_1)$ and $P(x_2, y_2)$ is given by:

$$\frac{y - y_1}{x - x_1} = \frac{y_2 - y_1}{x_2 - x_1}$$

This is the *two-point form* of a linear equation.

The equation of a line intersecting the x-axis at $(x_0, 0)$ and the y-axis at $(0, y_0)$ is given by:

$$\frac{x}{x_0} + \frac{y}{y_0} = 1$$

This is the *intercept form* of a linear equation.

The equation of a line with slope m intersecting the y-axis at $(0, b)$ is given by:

$$y = mx + b$$

This is the *slope-intercept* form of a linear equation.

Problems on linear equations:

A) Find the slope, the y-intercept, and the x-intercept of the equation $2x - 3y - 18 = 0$.

SOLUTION

The equation $2x - 3y - 18 = 0$ can be written in the form of the general linear equation, $ax + by = c$.

$$2x - 3y - 18 = 0$$

$$2x - 3y = 18$$

To find the slope and y-intercept, we derive them from the formula of the general linear equation $ax + by = c$. Dividing by b and solving for y, we obtain:

$$\frac{a}{b}x + y = \frac{c}{b}$$

$$y =$$

where $\dfrac{-a}{b}$ = slope and $\dfrac{c}{b}$ = y-intercept.

To find the x-intercept, solve for x and let $y = 0$:

$$x = \frac{c}{a} - \frac{b}{a}y$$

$$x = \frac{c}{a}$$

In this form we have $a = 2$, $b = -3$, and $c = 18$. Thus,

$$\text{slope} = -\frac{a}{b} = -\frac{2}{-3} = \frac{2}{3}$$

$$y\text{-intercept} = \frac{c}{b} = \frac{18}{-3} = -6$$

$$x\text{-intercept} = \frac{c}{a} = \frac{18}{2} = 9$$

B) Find the equation for the line passing through $(3, 5)$ and $(-1, 2)$.

SOLUTION

A): We use the two-point form with $(x_1, y_1) = (3, 5)$ and $(x_2, y_2) = (-1, 2)$. Then

$$\frac{y - y_1}{x - x_1} = \frac{y_2 - y_1}{x_2 - x_1}$$

$$\frac{y_2 - y_1}{x_2 - x_1} = \frac{2 - 5}{-1 - 3} \qquad \text{thus} \qquad \frac{y - 5}{x - 3} = \frac{-3}{-4}$$

Cross-multiply, $\quad -4(y-5) = -3(x-3)$.

Distribute, $\quad -4y + 20 \quad = \quad -3x + 9$

Place in general form, $\quad 3x - 4y = -11$.

Solution B): Does the same equation result if we let $(x_1, y_1) = (-1, 2)$ and $(x_2, y_2) = (3, 5)$?

$$\frac{y_2 - y_1}{x_2 - x_1} = \frac{5-2}{3-(-1)} \qquad \text{thus} \qquad \frac{y-2}{x+1} = \frac{3}{4}$$

Cross-multiply, $\quad 4(y-2) = 3(x+1)$

Distribute $\quad 4y - 8 = 3x + 3$

Place in general form, $\quad 3x - 4y = -11$.

Hence, either replacement results in the same equation. Keep in mind that the coefficient of the x-term should always be positive.

C) (a) Find the equation of the line passing through (2,5) with slope 3.

(b) Suppose a line passes through the y-axis at (0,b). How can we write the equation if the point-slope form is used?

Solution C): (a) In the point-slope form, let $x_1 = 2$, $y_1 = 5$, and $m = 3$. The point-slope form of a line is:

$$y - y_1 = m(x - x_1)$$

$$y - 5 = 3(x - 2)$$

$$y - 5 = 3x - 6 \qquad \text{Distributive property}$$

$$y = 3x - 1 \qquad \text{Addition property}$$

(b) $y - b = m(x - 0)$

$$y = mx + b.$$

Notice that this is the slope-intercept form for the equation of a line.

Inequalities

An inequality is a statement in which the value of one quantity or expression is greater than ($>$), less than ($<$), greater than or equal to ($\geq$), less than or equal to ($\leq$), or not equal to ($\neq$) that of another.

Example

$5 > 4$

The expression above means that the value of 5 is greater than the value of 4.

A **conditional inequality** is an inequality whose validity depends on the values of the variables in the statement. That is, certain values of the variables will make the statement true, and others will make it false. $3 - y > 3 + y$ is a conditional inequality for the set of real numbers, since it is true for any replacement less than 0 and false for all others.

$x + 5 > x + 2$ is an **absolute inequality** for the set of real numbers, meaning that for any real value x, the expression on the left is greater than the expression on the right.

$y + 3 < y + 2$ is inconsistent for all real y values. A sentence is **inconsistent** if it is always false when its variables assume allowable values.

The solution of a given inequality in one variable x consists of all values of x for which the inequality is true.

The graph of an inequality in one variable is represented by either a ray or a line segment on the real number line.

The endpoint is not a solution if the variable is strictly less than or greater than a particular value.

Example

$x > 2$

2 is not a solution and should be represented as shown.

The endpoint is a solution if the variable is either (1) less than or equal to or (2) greater than or equal to a particular value.

Example

$5 > x \geq 2$

In this case 2 is a solution and should be represented as shown.

Properties of Inequalities

If x and y are real numbers, then one and only one of the following statements is true:

$x > y$, $x = y$, or $x < y$

This is the order property of real numbers.

If a, b, and c are real numbers:

A) If $a < b$ and $b < c$, then $a < c$.

B) If $a > b$ and $b > c$, then $a > c$.

This is the **transitive property of inequalities.**

If a, b, and c are real numbers and $a > b$, then $a + c > b + c$ and $a - c > b - c$. This is the **addition property of inequality**.

Two inequalities are said to have the same **sense** if their signs of inequality point in the same direction.

The sense of an inequality remains the same if both sides are multiplied or divided by the same positive real number.

Example

$4 > 3$

If we multiply both sides by 5, we will obtain

$4 \times 5 > 3 \times 5$

$20 > 15$

The sense of the inequality does not change.

The sense of an inequality becomes opposite if each side is multiplied or divided by the same negative real number.

Example

$4 > 3$

If we multiply both sides by -5, we would obtain

$4 \times (-5) < 3 \times (-5)$

$-20 < -15$

The sense of the inequality becomes opposite.

If $a > b$ and a, b, and n are positive real numbers, then

$a^n > b^n$ and $a^{-n} < b^{-n}$

If $x > y$ and $q > p$, then $x + q > y + p$.

If $x > y > 0$ and $q > p > 0$, then $xq > yp$.

Inequalities that have the same solution set are called **equivalent inequalities**.

PROBLEM

Solve the inequality $2x + 5 > 9$.

SOLUTION

$2x + 5 + (-5) > 9 + (-5)$	Adding -5 to both sides
$2x + 0 > 9 + (-5)$	Additive inverse property
$2x > 9 + (-5)$	Additive identity property
$2x > 4$	Combining terms
$\dfrac{1}{2}(2x) > \dfrac{1}{2} \times 4$	Multiplying both sides by $^1/_2$
$x > 2$	

The solution set is

$$X = \{x \mid 2x + 5 > 9 \}$$
$$= \{x \mid x > 2\}$$

(that is, all x, such that x is greater than 2).

PROBLEM

Solve the inequality $4x + 3 < 6x + 8$.

SOLUTION

In order to solve the inequality $4x + 3 < 6x + 8$, we must find all values of x which make it true. Thus, we wish to obtain x alone on one side of the inequality.

Add -3 to both sides.

$$
\begin{array}{rcl}
4x + 3 & < & 6x + 8 \\
-3 & & -3 \\
\hline
4x & < & 6x + 5
\end{array}
$$

Add $-6x$ to both sides.

$$4x < 6x + 5$$
$$-6x \quad -6x$$
$$-2x < \qquad 5$$

In order to obtain x alone, we must divide both sides by (-2). Recall that dividing an inequality by a negative number reverses the inequality sign, hence

$$\frac{-2x}{-2} > \frac{5}{-2}$$

Cancelling $^{-2}/_{-2}$, we obtain $x > -\,^{5}/_{2}$.

Thus, our solution is $\{x : x > -\,^{5}/_{2}\}$ (the set of all x such that x is greater than $-\,^{5}/_{2}$).

Equations

An equation is defined as a statement of equality of two separate expressions known as members.

A *conditional equation* is an equation that is true for only certain values of the unknowns (variables) involved.

Example

$y + 6 = 11$ is true for $y = 5$.

An equation that is true for all permissible values of the unknown in question is called an identity. For example, $2x = \dfrac{4}{2}x$ is an identity of $x \in$ R, i.e., it is true for all reals.

The values of the variables that satisfy a conditional equation are called solutions of the conditional equation; the set of all such values is known as the solution set.

The solution to an equation $f(x) = 0$ is called the root of the equation.

Equations with the same solutions are said to be equivalent equations.

A statement of equality between two expressions containing rational coefficients and whose exponents are integers is called a rational integral equation. The degree of the equation is given by the term with highest power, as shown below:

$$a_n x^n + a_{n-1}x^{n-1} + a_{n-2}x^{n-2} + \ldots + a_1 x + a_0 = 0$$

where $a_n \neq 0$, the a_1, $i = 1 \ldots n$ are rational constant coefficients and n is a positive integer.

PROBLEM

Solve $3x - 5 = 4$ for x.

SOLUTION

Since $3x - 5 = 4$ is to be solved for x, isolate x on one side of the equation. First, add 5 to both sides of the equation.

$$3x - 5 + 5 = 4 + 5 \qquad (1)$$

Since $-5 + 5 = 0$ and $4 + 5 = 9$, equation (1) reduces to:

$$3x = 9. \qquad (2)$$

Since it is desired to get the term x isolated on one side of the equation, divide both sides of Equation (2) by 3.

$$\frac{3x}{3} = \frac{9}{3} \qquad (3)$$

Since $\frac{3x}{3}$ reduces to $1x$, and since $\frac{9}{3}$ reduces to 3, Equation (3) becomes: $1x = 3$. Since $1x = x$, $x = 3$. Therefore, the equation has been solved for x.

Check: By substituting $x = 3$ into the original equation, we have

$$3(3) - 5 \overset{?}{=} 4$$
$$9 - 5 \overset{?}{=} 4$$
$$4 = 4$$

Note that, upon substitution of the solution into the original equation, the equation is reduced to the identity $4 = 4$.

PROBLEM

Solve the equation $6x - 3 = 7 + 5x$.

SOLUTION

To solve for x in the equation $6x - 3 = 7 + 5x$, we wish to obtain an equivalent equation in which each term in one member involves x, and each term in the other member is a constant. If we add $(-5x)$ to both members, then only one side of the equation will have an x term:

$$6x - 3 + (-5x) = 7 + 5x + (-5x)$$
$$6x + (-5x) - 3 = 7 + 0$$
$$x - 3 = 7$$

Now, adding 3 to both sides of the equation, we obtain,

$$x - 3 + 3 = 7 + 3$$
$$x + 0 = 10$$
$$x = 10$$

Thus, our solution is $x = 10$. Now we check this value.

Check: Substitute 10 for x in the original equation:

$$6x - 3 = 7 + 5x$$
$$6(10) - 3 = 7 + 5(10)$$
$$60 - 3 = 7 + 50$$
$$57 = 57$$

PROBLEM

> Solve, justifying each step: $3x - 8 = 7x + 8$.

SOLUTION

$$3x - 8 = 7x + 8$$

Adding 8 to both members	$3x - 8 + 8 = 7x + 8 + 8$
Additive inverse property	$3x + 0 = 7x + 16$
Additive identity property	$3x = 7x + 16$
Adding $(-7x)$ to both members	$3x - 7x = 7x + 16 - 7x$
Commuting	$-4x = 7x - 7x + 16$
Additive inverse property	$-4x = 0 + 16$
Additive identity property	$-4x = 16$
Dividing both sides by -4	$\dfrac{-4x}{-4} = \dfrac{16}{-4}$
	$x = -4$

Check: Replacing x by -4 in the original equation:

$$3x - 8 = 7x + 8$$
$$3(-4) - 8 = 7(-4) + 8$$
$$-12 - 8 = -28 + 8$$
$$-20 = -20$$

$$*\quad 3x - 8 = 7x + 8$$
$$-3x \qquad -3x$$
$$\overline{\qquad\qquad\qquad}$$
$$-8 = 4x + 8$$
$$+8 \qquad -8$$
$$\overline{\qquad\qquad\qquad}$$
$$\frac{-16}{4} = \frac{4x}{4}$$
$$-4 = x$$

MATH REVIEW EXERCISES

ANSWER KEY

Exercise 1 – Exponents

1. (A)	2. (D)	3. (B)	4. (B)
5. (C)	6. (B)	7. (C)	8. (A)
9. (D)			

Exercise 2 – Ratios and Proportions

1. (B) 2. (A) 3. (A)

Exercise 3 – Rate

1. (C) 2. (A) 3. (A)

Exercise 4 – Discount

1. (D) 2. (C) 3. (B)

Exercise 5 – Points, Lines, and Angles

1. (B)	2. (A)	3. (C)	4. (B)
5. (C)	6. (B)		

Exercise 6 – Quadrilaterals

1. (D) 2. (C) 3. (A)

Exercise 7 – Circles

1. (B) 2. (C) 3. (A)

Exercise 8 – Coordinate Geometry

1. (A) 2. (C) 3. (A)

Exercise 9 – Linear Equations

1. (D) 2. (D) 3. (B)

NEW JERSEY
HSPA
High School Proficiency Assessment in
Mathematics

Practice
Test 1

REFERENCE INFORMATION FOR THE HSPA

12 inches = 1 foot
3 feet = 1 yard
36 inches = 1 yard
5,280 feet = 1 mile
1,760 yards = 1 mile

100 centimeters = 1 meter
1000 meters = 1 kilometer

1000 milliliters (mL) =
1 liter (L)

60 seconds = 1 minute
60 minutes = 1 hour
24 hours = 1 day
7 days = 1 week
52 weeks = 1 year

1000 watt hours =
1 kilowatt hour

1000 milligrams = 1 gram
100 centigrams = 1 gram
10 grams = 1 dekagram
1000 grams = 1 kilogram

8 fluid ounces = 1 cup
2 cups = 1 pint
2 pints = 1 quart
4 quarts = 1 gallon

Rectangle

Area = lw
Perimeter = $2(l + w)$

Parallelogram

Area = bh

$\pi \approx 3.14$ or $\frac{22}{7}$

Circle

Area = πr^2
Circumference = $2\pi r$

Sphere

Volume = $\frac{4}{3}\pi r^3$

Rectangular Prism

Volume = lwh
Surface Area = $2lw + 2wh + 2lh$

Triangle

Area = $\frac{1}{2}bh$

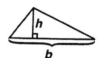

Pythagorean Formula

$c^2 = a^2 + b^2$

Trapezoid

Area = $\frac{1}{2}(b_1 + b_2)h$

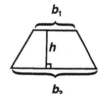

Cylinder

Volume = $\pi r^2 h$

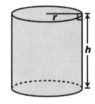

Cone

Volume = $\frac{1}{3}\pi r^2 h$

The sum of the measures of the interior angles of a triangle = 180°

The measure of a circle is 360° or 2π radians

Distance = rate $*$ time   Interest = principal $*$ rate $*$ time

Compound Interest Formula: $A = p\left(1+\frac{r}{k}\right)^{kt}$

A = amount after t years; p = principal; r = annual interest rate; t = number of years;
k = number of times compounded per year

The number of combinations of n elements taken r at a time is given by $\dfrac{n!}{(n-r)!r!}$

The number of permutations of n elements taken r at a time is given by $\dfrac{n!}{(n-r)!}$

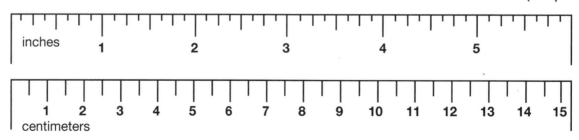

HSPA
Mathematics

Practice Test 1*
(See page 205 for answer sheets.)

TIME: 120 Minutes (Note: In the actual test administration, students will be given a brief break after each section.)
48 Questions

DIRECTIONS: Record your answers on the answer sheets provided.

Part I

1. $(4 \times 10^{15}) \times (2 \times 10^8) =$

   (A) 8×10^7 (C) 2×10^{23}

   (B) 8×10^{22} (D) 8×10^{23}

2. A piggy bank contains only nickels and dimes. In all there are 42 coins with a total value of $3.85. How many nickels are in the piggy bank?

   (A) 3   (C) 17

   (B) 7   (D) 35

3. Use the table to answer the question.

WORLD POPULATION AVERAGE
(Billions)

Year	Developed Countries	Developing Countries
1950	0.8	1.8
1960	0.9	2.4
1970	1.2	2.9
1980	1.3	3.0
1990	1.37	4.2
2000	1.4	5.2

---

* The HSPA test is given over a two- or three-day period. Testing times and section lengths are approximate, and will vary from administration to administration.

Between 1960 and 2000 the average world population in undeveloped countries increased by

(A) .5 billion.

(C) 2.8 billion.

(B) .6 billion.

(D) 3.4 billion.

4. In the diagram below, lines l_1 and l_2 are parallel.

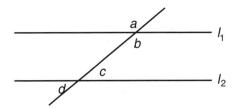

Which of the following is equal to $a + b + c + d$?

(A) 120°

(C) 240°

(B) 180°

(D) 360°

5. Richard earns $10 per hour, and Mark earns $8 per hour. How long must Mark work in order to earn the same amount of money as Richard earns in five hours?

(A) 5 hours, 45 min.

(C) 6 hours, 15 min.

(B) 6 hours

(D) 6 hours, 25 min.

6. Which of the following shows that the length (L) varies inversely as the cube of the width (w)?

(A) $L = \dfrac{w^3}{k}$

(C) $L = \dfrac{k}{w^3}$

(B) $kw^3 = L$

(D) $kL = w^3$

7. Use the diagram to answer the question.

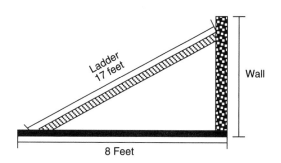

A 17-foot ladder leans against a wall. If the ladder is 8 feet from the base of the wall, how far is it from the bottom of the wall to the top of the ladder?

(A) 5 feet

(C) $2\sqrt{34}$ feet

(B) 9 feet

(D) 15 feet

8. A circular region rotated 360° around its diameter (serving as an axis) generates a

(A) cube.

(B) rectangular parallelepiped.

(C) cone.

(D) sphere.

9. In an apartment building there are 9 apartments having terraces for every 16 apartments. If the apartment building has a total of 144 apartments, how many apartments have terraces?

(A) 63

(C) 102

(B) 81

(D) 137

10. How many factors are there for the number 300, including 1 and 300? (Use only positive integers)

(A) 15

(C) 17

(B) 16

(D) 18

11. At the Sleep-Easy Motel, a senior citizen is given a $10-per-night discount, calculated by taking the cost of each night's lodging, adding an 8% sales tax, then deducting $10 per night. At the Rest-Well Motel, a senior citizen is also given a $10-per-night discount. The discount is first applied to the cost of each night's lodging; then the 8% sales tax is added. At either motel, one night's lodging (before discounts) costs $90.

    • What is the cost for a senior citizen to stay at the Sleep-Easy Motel for 4 nights?

    • What is the cost for a senior citizen to stay at the Rest-Well Motel for 4 nights?

    • In order for the cost to be the same at each motel, how much of a discount, in dollars and cents, should be offered at the Rest-Well Motel?

12. Suppose that a certain municipality uses the equation $y = 3(x - 50) + 30$ to determine the fine assessed a car which exceeds the 50 mph speed limit. Let x = speed of the car (in mph) and y = corresponding fine in dollars.

    • What is the fine for traveling at 55 mph?

    • If the fine is $126, what is the speed of the car?

    • If car A travels at 60 mph and car B travels at 90 mph, then car B is traveling 50% faster than car A. However, the fine for car B is what percent higher than that of car A?

Part II

13. The number missing in the sequence 2, 6, 12, 20, x, 42, 56 is

    (A) 24.   (C) 30.

    (B) 29.   (D) 36.

14. Examine the pattern sequence and answer the question.

    1 z 3 w 9 __?__ 27 q 81

    What is the missing symbol?

    (A) 13   (C) t

    (B) s (D) u

15. A rectangle is divided into three squares, as shown in the diagram. If the long side of the rectangle is equal to 12 cm, what is the area of one of the squares?

    (A) 8 cm²   (C) 32 cm²

    (B) 16 cm²   (D) 64 cm²

16. A cardboard box has a volume of 24 ft³. If the box is 3 ft. long and 2 ft. wide, what is the height of the box?

    (A) 4 ft.   (C) 6 ft.

    (B) 5 ft.   (D) 7 ft.

17. Each employee of the Pepperland Company has a seven-digit ID number. When read as a whole number, it must be divisible by 8. Also, the last (rightmost) two digits cannot be the same. How many employees' numbers could read 57894__?

    (A) 10   (C) 12

    (B) 11   (D) 13

18. At Butcher Bob's Meat Pit, each hamburger comes with any of the following: tomato, onion, lettuce, and/or cheese. On Saturdays, a customer can get a fabulous prize when buying a hamburger with at least one of these four items. How many different hamburgers qualify for a fabulous prize?

    (A) 15   (C) 17

    (B) 16   (D) 18

    Question 21 refers to the following diagram. Use the following drawing for question 21.

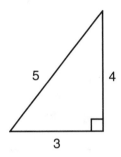

19. Which one of the triangles shown below is NOT similar to the triangle given above? (Note: drawings are not to scale.)

(A)

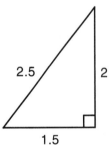

(C)

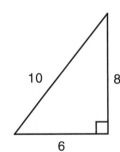

(B)

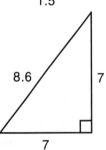

(D)

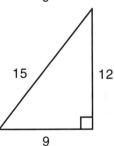

20. Which of the following vectors is equal to vector **MN** if $M = (2, 1)$ and $N = (3, -4)$?

    (A) vector **AB**, where $A = (1, -1)$ and $B = (2, 3)$

    (B) vector **CD**, where $C = (-4, 5)$ and $D = (-3, 10)$

    (C) vector **EF**, where $E = (3, -2)$ and $F = (4, -7)$

    (D) vector **GH**, where $G = (3, 2)$ and $H = (7, -4)$

21. A rectangular box is to be filled with boxes of candy. The rectangular box measures 4 feet long, 3 feet wide, and $2^1/_2$ feet deep. If a box of candy weighs approximately 3 pounds per cubic foot, what will the weight of the rectangular box be when the box is filled to the top with candy?

    (A) 10 pounds   (C) 36 pounds

    (B) 12 pounds   (D) 90 pounds

22. Point P, whose coordinates are $(3, 2)$, is reflected through the y-axis to give a new point, P'. Next, P' undergoes a translation two units to the left, giving another new point, P''. What are the coordinates of point P''?

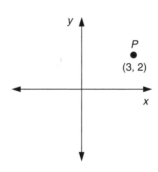

    (A) $(-3, 2)$ (C) $(1, -2)$

    (B) $(-5, 2)$ (D) $(-2, -3)$

23. Two trucks leave a warehouse at the same time. Truck A travels east at 50 mph and Truck B travels north at 60 mph.

    • If Truck A reaches its destination in 2 hours and Truck B reaches its destination in 3 hours, how many miles apart will they be?

    • Suppose Truck C will travel from Truck A's destination to Truck B's destination. If Truck C travels at 40 mph for half the distance of this trip, how fast will it need to travel for the remaining distance in order to complete its entire trip in 4 hours? (Figure to the nearest 1/10 mph.)

24. John is thinking of a two-digit number. It is a prime number which is 3 less than a perfect square. Also, when its digits are reversed, it becomes a perfect square. What is the one possible number? Explain.

Part III

25. The sum of 3 angles of a triangle is 180°. The second angle is 11° less than the first angle. The third angle is twice the measure of the first angle increased by 3. If x represents the number of degrees in the first angle, which equation correctly represents the relationship among the three angles?

    (A) $x + (11 - x) + (2x + 3) = 180$

    (B) $x + (x - 11) + 2(x + 3) = 180$

    (C) $x + (x - 11) + (2x + 3) = 180$

    (D) $x + (x - 11) + (2x - 3) = 180$

Use the chart below for questions 26–28.

G.P.A.	2.0	2.4	3.2	3.5	3.8	4.0
Earnings (in thousands of dollars)	15	20	30	28	35	40

26. For which G.P.A. would the earnings be considered an outlier?

    (A) 2.7   (C) 3.5

    (B) 3.2   (D) 3.8

27. If there exists an exact linear relationship between a G.P.A. of 2.4 and a G.P.A. of 3.2, what would the corresponding earnings (in thousands of dollars) be for a G.P.A. of 3.0?

    (A) 26   (C) 28.5

    (B) 27.5   (D) 29

28. If there were an exact linear relationship between a G.P.A. of 2.0 and a G.P.A. of 4.0, what would be the difference (in thousands of dollars) between the actual earnings corresponding to a G.P.A. of 3.8 and the theoretical earnings for this G.P.A., based on exact linearity?

    (A) 2.5   (C) 4.5

    (B) 3.5   (D) 5.5

29. Read the bar graph and answer the question.

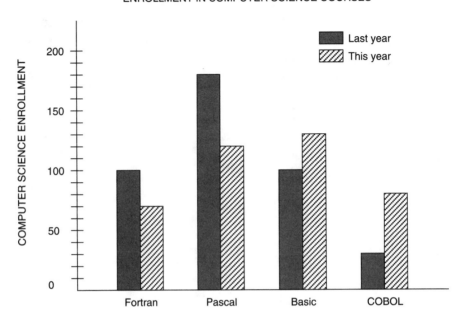

ENROLLMENT IN COMPUTER SCIENCE COURSES

Which computer science course showed the greatest increase in enrollment between last year and this year?

(A) Fortran

(C) Basic

(B) Pascal

(D) COBOL

30. A poker hand consists of 5 cards from a deck of 52 cards. How many different poker hands are possible which contain exactly 3 diamonds?

(A) 193,336

(C) 211,926

(B) 199,920

(D) 229,354

31. What percent of 85 is 17?

(A) 5%

(C) 20%

(B) 14 $\frac{9}{20}$%

(D) 68%

32. A carpenter is building a big recreation room that is 625 square feet in area, and he must decide how to apportion each section of the room. He has decided to set aside 30% of the room for the Baby Grand Piano and an additional 46.7 square feet for a stage. How much of the room is set aside for the Baby Grand Piano and stage?

    (A) 76.7 square feet   (C) 548.3 square feet

    (B) 234.2 square feet   (D) 610.99 square feet

33. John wishes to contribute $2,500 to his favorite charities, A and B, in the ratio of 2 to 3. The amount he should contribute to charity A is

    (A) $500.   (C) $1,250.

    (B) $1,000.   (D) $1,500.

34. Sam finds that his monthly commission in dollars, C, can be calculated by the equation $C = 270g - 3g^2$, where g is the number of goods he sells for the company. In January, he sold 30 goods; and in February, he sold 40 goods. How much additional commission did Sam make in February over January?

    (A) $600   (C) $6,000

    (B) $5,400   (D) $11,400

35. Tim and Wanda work in a certain company. Tim works a shift of 11 consecutive days, then gets 1 day off. Wanda works a shift of 19 consecutive days, then gets 1 day off.

    • If Tim and Wanda both start work on January 1, when is the first day when both will be off work on the same day? Assume 28 days in February.

    • If Tim is paid $85 per day, how much per day should Wanda make so that each person will get the same pay per shift? Include the day off as part of the shift.

36. Adam, Brenda and Carol are playing a game in which each player shoots basketball foul shots. The players are of different abilities, dictating that each have a specific equation to determine the number of points (y) based on number of foul shots made. Here are the equations for each player:

    Adam: $y = 2x$

    Brenda: $y = x + 1$

    Carol: $y = 5x - 2$

- Which player has the least ability?

- If Brenda makes 22 foul shots, how many foul shots will Carol need to make to equal Brenda's point total?

- Adam takes a total of 40 foul shots, but only makes 60% of them for points. How many successful foul shots does Brenda need to make to score as many points as Adam?

Part IV

37. Which one of the following numbers has exactly two prime factors?

    (A) 13   (C) 18

    (B) 15   (D) 20

38. $\triangle ABC$ is situated on an *xy*-coordinate plane with locations as follows: A: (2, 1), B: (1, 4), C: (6, 0). If the triangle is reflected over the *x*-axis so that *A* becomes *A'*, *B* becomes *B'*, and *C* becomes *C'*, what is the slope of $\overline{A'B'}$?

    (A) –3   (C) 1/3

    (B) –1/3   (D) 3

39. In a class of students, two-fifths are men. If two-thirds of the women have blond hair and one-half of all the students have blond hair, what fraction of the students are men who do NOT have blond hair?

    (A) 1/10   (C) 3/10

    (B) 1/5   (D) 2/5

40. In $\triangle PQR$, $PQ = 8$ and $PR = 10$. The lengths of all three sides are integers. If $m \angle P > 90°$, what is the MINIMUM value of the perimeter of $\triangle PQR$?

    (A) 31   (C) 35

    (B) 33   (D) 37

41. In a certain school district, the teacher–student ratio is 1:25. Currently, the school district has 3,150 students. If the student enrollment increases by 20%, how many additional teachers must be hired to reduce the teacher–student ratio to 1:18?

    (A) 210   (C) 84

    (B) 175   (D) 49

42. What is the units digit of the number $3^{1,000,000}$?

    (A) 1   (C) 7

    (B) 3   (D) 9

43. The probability that it will rain tomorrow is .60, and the probability that Joe will go bowling is .30. Assuming that these events are independent, what is the probability that exactly one of these events will occur?

(A) .18

(C) .72

(B) .54

(D) .82

44. A scale model of a rectangular plot of land is 14 inches long by 8 inches wide. If the actual length of this plot of land is 224 feet, what is its actual area, in square feet?

(A) 704

(C) 25,088

(B) 1,040

(D) 28,672

45. Suppose a sequence of numbers a_i is given as follows: $a_1 = 1$, $a_2 = 2$, $a_i = (a_{i-2})(a_{i-1})$ for all each $i \geq 3$. What is the value of a_6?

(A) 32

(C) 16

(B) 24

(D) 6

46. For 5 consecutive days, the price of a lamp in Jill's store is reduced by 10% from the previous day's price. At the end of the fifth day, by what percentage will the price of the lamp have been reduced from its initial price?

(A) 64

(C) 50

(B) 59

(D) 41

47. In the town of Niceville, a local lottery is held once a year for the residents. Lottery tickets cost 50 cents apiece. Each lottery ticket contains four numbers, from 1 to 20. The lottery machine will select six numbers from 1 to 20. A winning ticket, worth $100, will contain four of the six numbers chosen by the machine.

- How much money would a person need to spend to buy every possible combination of four numbers?

- What is the probability, to the nearest ten-thousandth, that a person will select four correct numbers?

- To the nearest ten-thousandth, what is the probability that a ticket has NO correct numbers?

48. In the town of Moneyville, a wage tax is imposed on individuals who work there. If a person is a resident of Moneyville, the tax is $2 for the first $200 of the gross amount of the paycheck, and 0.6% for any gross amount over $200. For a nonresident, the tax is $5 for the first $100 of the gross amount of the paycheck, and 1.2% for any gross amount over $100.

   • If James lives and works in Moneyville, how much tax will he pay per week if his weekly gross salary is $800?

   • If Marianne works in Moneyville but is not a resident, how much tax will she pay per week if her weekly gross salary is $600?

   • Linda is a new employee for one of the companies in Moneyville. Currently, she is a nonresident. If her weekly gross salary will be $1,000, how much less tax will she pay for an entire year if she becomes a resident of Moneyville? (Assume that her weekly gross salary will remain $1,000.)

HSPA
PRACTICE TEST 1

ANSWER KEY

MATHEMATICS

Part I

1.	(D)	5.	(C)	9.	(B)
2.	(B)	6.	(C)	10.	(D)
3.	(C)	7.	(D)	11.	Open-Ended
4.	(D)	8.	(D)	12.	Open-Ended

Part II

13.	(C)	17.	(B)	21.	(D)
14.	(C)	18.	(A)	22.	(B)
15.	(B)	19.	(B)	23.	Open-Ended
16.	(A)	20.	(C)	24.	Open-Ended

Part III

25.	(C)	29.	(D)	33.	(B)
26.	(C)	30.	(C)	34.	(A)
27.	(B)	31.	(C)	35.	Open-Ended
28.	(A)	32.	(B)	36.	Open-Ended

Part IV

37.	(B)	41.	(C)	45.	(A)
38.	(D)	42.	(B)	46.	(D)
39.	(C)	43.	(B)	47.	Open-Ended
40.	(A)	44.	(D)	48.	Open-Ended

DETAILED EXPLANATIONS
OF ANSWERS

TEST 1

Part I

1. **(D)**

$$(4 \times 10^{15}) \times (2 \times 10^8) = (4 \times 2) \times (10^{15} \times 10^8)$$
$$= 8 \times 10^{15+8}$$

In multiplication of terms with the same base, we add exponents.

$$= 8 \times 10^{23}$$

Answer choice (A) is incorrect because exponents were subtracted.

$$(4 \times 10^{15}) \times (2 \times 10^8) = (4 \times 2) \times (10^{15} \times 10^8)$$
$$= 8 \times (10^{15-8})$$
$$= 8 \times 10^7$$

Answer choice (B) is incorrect because the exponents were incorrectly added.

$$(4 \times 10^{15}) \times (2 \times 10^8) = (4 \times 2) \times (10^{15} \times 10^8)$$
$$= 8 \times (10^{15+8})$$
$$= 8 \times 10^{22}$$

Answer choice (C) is incorrect due to a subtraction of the values 4 and 2.

$$(4 \times 10^{15}) \times (2 \times 10^8) = (4 - 2) \times (10^{15} \times 10^8)$$
$$= 2 \times (10^{15+8})$$
$$= 2 \times 10^{23}$$

2. **(B)**

Let x = number of nickels, then

$.05x$ = monetary value of the number of nickels

Let y = number of dimes, then

$.10y$ = monetary value of the number of dimes

Since there are 42 coins in the bank, and the bank contains only nickels and dimes, then

$$\text{number of nickels} \quad + \quad \text{number of dimes} \quad = \quad \text{42 coins, or}$$

$$\downarrow \qquad\qquad\qquad\qquad \downarrow$$

$$x \qquad + \qquad y \qquad = \qquad 42$$

Since the total monetary value of the coins in the bank is $3.85, then

$$\text{monetary value of} \quad \text{monetary value of} \quad = \quad \$3.85, \text{ or}$$
$$\text{nickels} \quad + \quad \text{dimes}$$

$$\downarrow \qquad\qquad\qquad\qquad \downarrow$$

$$.05x \qquad + \qquad .10y \qquad = \qquad \$3.85$$

Since the problem asks us to determine the number of nickels written in terms of x, we want the equation

$$.05x + .10y = \$3.85$$

(or multiplying through by 100, each term, in order to move the decimal points two places to the right, we get)

$$5x + 10y = 385$$

to be written in terms of x, so that "y" is replaced by the term $10y$.

Solving for y in the equation $x + y = 42$, we subtract x from both sides to get

$$
\begin{aligned}
x + y &= 42 \\
-x \qquad\quad &\quad -x \\
y &= 42 - x
\end{aligned}
$$

Substitute $y = 42 - x$ in the equation

$$5x + 10y = 385$$

This gives us

$$
\begin{aligned}
y &= 42 - x \\
5x + 10y &= 385 \\
5x + 10(42 - x) &= 385 \quad \text{substituting for } y \\
5x + 420 - 10x &= 385 \quad \text{use distributive law} \\
-5x + 420 &= 385 \quad \text{combine like terms} \\
-420 \qquad\quad &\quad -420 \\
-5x &= -35 \quad \text{transpose the constant} \\
-5 \qquad\qquad &\quad -5 \quad \text{divide by the coefficient of } x \text{ on the left} \\
&\qquad\qquad\qquad \text{side of the equation} \\
x &= 7
\end{aligned}
$$

Answer choice (A) is incorrect because the total number of coins was changed to 40.

$$(x)(.05) + (40 - x)(.10) = \$3.85$$

$$(.05x) + 4.00 - (.10x) = \$3.85$$

$$-.05x = -.15$$

$$x = 3$$

Answer choice (C) is incorrect based on a guess of 30 dimes making $3.00 and 17 nickels making a total of $3.85, but with a wrong total number of coins.

$$30(.10) + 17(.05) = \$3.85, \quad 30 + 17 \neq 42$$

Answer choice (D) is incorrect because it refers to the number of dimes.

$$(42 - x)(.05) + x(.10) = 3.85$$

$$2.10 - .05(x) + .10(x) = 3.85$$

$$.05x = 1.75$$

$$x = 35 = \# \text{ of dimes}$$

3. **(C)**   The world population average in developing countries in 1960 was 2.4 billion. As shown in the table, the world population average in developing countries in 2000 will be 5.2 billion. Therefore, the average world population in developing countries increased by

5.2 billion – 2.4 billion = 2.8 billion

Answer (A) is wrong because data from developed countries was used: 1.4 billion – .9 billion = .5 billion. Answer (D) is wrong because the data from 1950 was used: 5.2 – 1.8 = 3.4 billion. Answer (B) is wrong because the data was taken from 1950 and 2000 of developed countries: 1.4 – .8 = .6 billion.

4. **(D)**   Look at the unlabeled angle to the right of angle *a*. This angle must be equal to angle *c*, since these two are corresponding angles.

Next look at the unlabeled angle below angle *a*. This angle must be equal to angle *d*, since these two are corresponding angles.

These observations allow us to re-draw the diagram as follows:

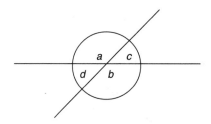

Even though we do not know the measures of *a, b, c,* or *d,* we see that they form a complete circle, so their sum is 360°.

If you have difficulty seeing this, you can analyze the re-drawn diagram in a slightly different way. Observe that

1) $a + c = 180°$, since *a* and *c* are supplementary.

2) $b + d = 180°$, since *d* and *b* are supplementary.

Combining 1) and 2) gives

$$a + b + c + d = (a + c) + (d + b) = 180° + 180° = 360°.$$

The answer is (D).

5.   **(C)**   How much does Richard earn in five hours?

He earns $\dfrac{\$10}{1 \text{ hour}}$ (5 hours) = \$50.

For Mark to earn this same amount (\$50), he must work longer since he earns less per hour.

For Mark,

$$\frac{\$8}{1 \text{ hour}} (x \text{ hours}) = \$50.$$

$$8x = 50$$

$$x = \frac{50}{8}$$

$$= 6.25 \text{ hours}$$

Notice that none of the answer choices is given in decimal form. Thus, we need to convert .25 hour to minutes. .25 hour is the same as $^1/_4$ hour. Since an hour contains 60 minutes, $^1/_4$ hour contains $^1/_4$ (60 min.) = 15 min. Therefore, Mark must work 6 hours, 15 min.

The answer is (C).

6. **(C)**   If x and y vary inversely as each other and k is the constant of variation, then $xy = k$. So if length (L) varies inversely as the cube of the width (w^3) then

$$Lw^3 = k$$

Solving for L, we divide both sides of the equation $Lw^3 = k$ by w^3 as follows:

$$\frac{L\cancel{w^3}}{\cancel{w^3}} = \frac{k}{w^3}$$

$$L = \frac{k}{w^3}$$

Therefore, answer choices (A), (B), and (D) are incorrect.

7. **(D)**   The triangle in the diagram is a right triangle. If the triangle is a right triangle, the lengths of the sides satisfy the Pythagorean property, namely $a^2 + b^2 = c^2$, where a, b are the lengths of the legs of the right triangle and c is the length of the hypotenuse. Therefore,

$$a^2 + b^2 = c^2 \text{ translates to}$$

$$(\text{length of base})^2 + (\text{length of wall})^2 = (\text{length of ladder})^2$$

or
$$\begin{aligned}
8^2 + b^2 &= 17^2 \\
64 + b^2 &= 289 \quad \text{Solving for } b^2, \\
-64 \quad\quad & -64 \\
b^2 &= 225
\end{aligned}$$

and $b^2 = 225$ means to take the positive square root of both sides which yields $b = 15$ feet.

Answer choice (A) is incorrect due to the improper use of the Pythagorean property.

$$17 \text{ feet} + 8 \text{ feet} = 25 \text{ feet}$$

$$\sqrt{25} = 5 \text{ feet}$$

Answer choice (B) is incorrect due to the improper use of the Pythagorean property.

$$17 \text{ feet} - 8 \text{ feet} = 9 \text{ feet}$$

Answer choice (C) is also incorrect due to the improper use of the Pythagorean property.

8. **(D)** A sphere is formed when a circle is rotated 360° about its diameter (serving as an axis).

9. **(B)**

$$\frac{9 \text{ apartments with terraces}}{16 \text{ apartments}} = \frac{?}{144 \text{ apartments}}$$

Solving this proportion for the "?"

$$? = \frac{9 \text{ apartments} \times 144 \text{ apartments}}{16 \text{ apartments}} = \frac{1296 \text{ apartments}}{16 \text{ apartments}} = 81 \text{ apartments}$$

Answer (A) is incorrect because the number of apartments with terraces is 9, not $16 - 9$.

$$(144 \div 16) \times (16 - 9) = 9 \times 7 = 63$$

Answer (C) is incorrect due to a multiplication factor guess of 6.

$$144 - [(16 - 9) \times 6] = 102$$

Answer (D) is incorrect because the apartments were subtracted.

$$144 - (16 - 9) = 144 - 7 = 137 \text{ apartments}$$

10. **(D)** 18
Rewrite 300 as 2^2 times 3^1 times 5^2. The number of factors becomes the product of one more than each exponent, which means $(2+1)(1+1)(2+1) = (3)(2)(3) = 18$. Checking this result, the factors are: 1, 2, 3, 4, 5, 6, 10, 12, 15, 20, 25, 30, 50, 60, 75, 100, 150, 300.

11. At the Sleep-Easy Motel, 4 nights would cost $(4)(90)(1.08) - 40 = \$348.80$.

At the Rest-Well Motel, 4 nights would cost $(4)(90-10)(1.08) = \$345.60$.

One night at Sleep-Easy costs $(90)(1.08) - 10 = 87.20$. Let x = dollar discount at Rest-Well. Then:

$(90 - x)(1.08) = 87.20$. Solving, $x = \$9.26$ approximately.

12. At 55 mph, the fine is $3(55-50) + 30 = 45$ dollars.

$126 = 3(x - 50) + 30$. Solving, $x = 82$ mph.

At 60 mph, the fine is \$60, but at 90 mph, the fine is \$150. The percent increase is 150%.

Part II

13. **(C)**   The difference between the first two numbers is 4 (since 6 – 2 = 4); the difference between the second and third numbers is 6 (since 12 – 6 = 6), which is two more than the first difference; the difference between the third and fourth numbers is 8 (since 20 – 12 = 8), which is two more than the second difference. Following this pattern, the difference between the fourth and fifth numbers must be 10. Thus, the value of x is given by $x – 20 = 10$. Solving for x yields $x = 30$. So, the correct answer choice is (C). Similar analysis of each of the other choices will fail to provide a value for x such that it is a consistent distance in relation to the other numbers in the sequence.

14. **(C)**   The sequence alternates numbers with letters. Particularly, the number sequence represents powers of three, namely,

$$3^0 = 1, 3^1 = 3, 3^2 = 9, 3^3 = 27, 3^4 = 81$$

The letter sequence starts with the last letter of the alphabet, z, then deletes two letters preceding z — namely x, y. The next letter on the list is w; delete the two letters preceding w — namely u, v. Following this pattern, the next letter in the sequence is t, because, after deleting the two letters preceding t, we get the letter q.

   Diagrammatically, we start with q, deleting two subsequent letters until we end at the letter z:

$q \quad r \quad s \quad t \quad u \quad v \quad w \quad x \quad y \quad z$

$\uparrow$

   missing symbol in sequence

Since the sequence alternates numbers first, letters second, the missing symbol is a letter and must be t.

   Answer (A) is incorrect because the symbol needs to be a letter of the alphabet. Answers (B) and D) are incorrect because the symbol should be evenly separated by a number of letters so it falls into the midpoint of w and q.

15. **(B)**   First, you must determine if the three squares are congruent. Because they each have sides, S, equal to the short side of the rectangle, they must be congruent. However, the value of S is not given. We must calculate it by taking the length of the long side of the rectangle, 12 cm., and dividing it into three equal parts:

$$S = \frac{12}{3} \text{cm}$$

$$= 4 \text{ cm}$$

Now that we know that the squares have sides which are 4 cm. long, we can compute the area.

$$\text{Area of one square} = S \times S$$

$$= 4 \times 4$$

$$= 16 \text{ cm}^2$$

The answer is (B).

16. **(A)**   The formula for the volume of a rectangular solid is

$$\text{volume} = \text{length} \times \text{width} \times \text{height} \qquad (1)$$

or, $V = lwh$

The unknown in our problem is h, the height. Solving Equation (1) for h gives

$$h = \frac{V}{lw} \qquad (2)$$

Substituting $V = 24$, $l = 3$, and $w = 2$ into Equation (2) gives

$$h = \frac{24}{(3)(2)}$$

$$= \frac{24}{6}$$

$$= 4 \text{ ft.}$$

The answer is (A).

17. **(B)**   The actual possibilities for the last two digits are 08, 16, 24, 32, 40, 48, 56, 64, 72, 80, and 96.

18. **(A)**   The number of different hamburgers with 1, 2, 3 or 4 of the mentioned items is $_4C_1 + {_4C_2} + {_4C_3} + {_4C_4} = 4 + 6 + 4 + 1 = 15$.

19. **(B)**   Similar triangles are triangles whose corresponding angles are identical, and whose corresponding sides are in proportion.

How do we determine whether the corresponding sides of two different triangles are in proportion? We do this by looking for a single number which, when multiplied by each of the lengths of the sides of the first triangle, will yield each of the lengths of the sides of the second triangle. If such a number exists, the triangles are similar.

Let's test each of the answer choices to see if they are similar to the given 3, 4, 5 triangle:

Choice (A): Each side of this triangle is obtained by multiplying each side of the 3, 4, 5 triangle by $1/2$.

Choice (B): There is no single number which, when multiplied by each of the sides of the 3, 4, 5 triangle, will yield the sides of this triangle.

Choice (C): Each side of this triangle is obtained by multiplying each side of the 3, 4, 5 triangle by 2.

Choice (D): Each side of this triangle is obtained by multiplying each side of the 3, 4, 5 triangle by 3.

Thus, the triangle in choice (B) is the only one that is *not* similar to the original 3, 4, 5, triangle.

The answer is (B).

20. **(C)**   When adding vectors we add their respective components. First we must express the vectors as the distance from the origin to the given point. The point $M(2, 1)$ is the same as the vector **OM**. So we can represent the vector **MN** as the sum of the distance from the origin to M plus the distance from the origin to N. Thus,

$$\mathbf{MN} = \mathbf{MO} + \mathbf{ON}$$
$$= -\mathbf{MO} + \mathbf{ON}$$
$$= -(2, 1) + (3, -4)$$
$$= (1, -5)$$

Thus the distance and direction from M to N is the same as the distance from the origin to $(1, -5)$. Similarly,

$$\mathbf{AB} = -\mathbf{OA} + \mathbf{OB}$$
$$= -(1, -1) + (2, 3)$$
$$= (1, 4)$$
$$\mathbf{CD} = -(-4, 5) + (-3, 10)$$
$$= (1, 5)$$

$$\mathbf{EF} = -(3, -2) + (4, -7)$$

$$= (1, -5)$$

$$\mathbf{GH} = -(3, 2) + (7, -4)$$

$$= (4, -6)$$

Hence the vector **MN** is equivalent to the vector **EF**.

21. **(D)**

The volume of the rectangular box

$$= \text{(length)} \quad \text{(width)} \quad \text{(height)}$$

$$= \quad (4) \quad \times \quad (3) \quad \times \quad (2\tfrac{1}{2})$$

$$(12) \quad \quad \times \quad (2\tfrac{1}{2})$$

Writing quantities in fractional form:

$$= \frac{12}{1} \times \frac{5}{2}$$

Cancel and multiply numerators:

$$= \frac{6}{1} \times \frac{5}{1} = 30 \text{ cubic feet}$$

If each box of candy weighs approximately 3 pounds per cubic foot and there are 30 cubic feet in the rectangular box, the weight of the rectangular box is

(30 ~~cubic feet~~) (3 pounds/~~cubic foot~~) = 90 pounds

when the box is filled to the top with candy.

Answer (A) is wrong due to an error in computation.

4 ft × 3 ft × 2½ ft × ft³/3 pounds = 10 pounds

Answer (B) is wrong because it only considers the length of the box in the computation.

4 ft × 3 pounds/cubic foot = 12 pounds

Answer (C) is wrong because it deletes the height (deepness) from the computation.

4 ft × 3 ft × 3 pounds/cubic foot = 36 pounds

22. **(B)**   When we reflect point *P* across the *y*-axis, we imagine the *y*-axis as if it were a mirror.

The reflection of point *P* is another point, which we will label *P'*. *P'* is located on the opposite side of the *y*-axis from *P*. (*P* is in the first quadrant and *P'* is in the second quadrant.) Also, the distance from *P* to the *y*-axis is the same as the distance from *P'* to the *y*-axis. Thus, the coordinates of *P'* are (–3, 2). (See graph below.)

Now that we have found *P'*, we need to find *P''*. The problem tells us that *P'* undergoes a translation two units to the left to give *P''*. This movement would change the *x*-coordinate from –3 to –5, but would leave the y-coordinate unchanged. Thus, the coordinates of *P''* are (–5, 2). (See graph below.)

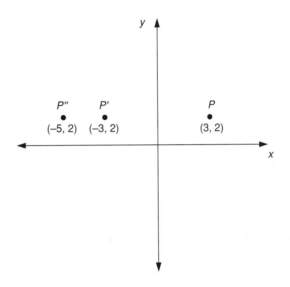

23.   Truck A travels (50)(2) = 100 miles east. Truck B travels (60)(3) = 180 miles north. Distance apart:

$$\sqrt{100^2 + 180^2} = \sqrt{42,400} \approx 206 \text{ miles}$$

Truck C travels at 40 mph for 103 miles, which requires 2.575 hrs. Then

4 – 2.575 = 1.425 hrs to cover the remaining miles.

Finally, 103/1.425 ≈ 72.3 miles/hr.

24.   61 is the number. The perfect squares under 121 are: 1, 4, 9, 16, 25, 36, 49, 64, 81, 100. Three less than these numbers: -2, 1, 6, 13, 22, 33, 46, 61, 78, 97. Of those, 13, 61 and 97 are prime. When 61 is reversed, it becomes 16, which is a perfect square.

Part III

25. **(C)**

x = number of degrees in the first angle. The second angle is **11°** less than the **first angle**; so the second angle = $x - 11$, where *less than* signifies subtraction, and the first angle (x) is the first term and 11° (or just 11) is the second term.

The third angle is twice **the measure of the first angle** increased by 3; so the third angle = $2x + 3$, where *twice* represents multiplication by 2 and *increased by* means addition.

Since the **sum** of the angles of a triangle equals 180°, then

$$\text{first angle} + \text{second angle} + \text{third angle} = 180°$$

$$\downarrow \qquad\qquad \downarrow \qquad\qquad \downarrow$$

$$x \quad + \quad (x - 11) \quad + \quad (2x + 3) = 180°$$

Answer choice (A) is wrong because of an error in interpretation of 11 less than x.

$$\angle 2 = (11 - x)$$

Answer choice (B) is wrong because of an error in interpretation of twice x increased by 3.

$$\angle 3 = 2(x + 3)$$

Answer choice (D) is wrong because of an error in interpretation of twice x increased by 3.

$$\angle 3 = (2x - 3)$$

26. **(C)** The earnings show an increase as the G.P.A. increases, except from a G.P.A. of 3.2 to a G.P.A. of 3.5.

27. **(B)** $(30 - 20) / (3.2 - 2.4) = 12.5$
Let x = earnings for a G.P.A. of 3.0. Then

$$(x - 20) / (3.0 - 2.4) = 12.5$$

Solving, $x = 27.5$.

28. **(A)**

$(40 - 15) / (4.0 - 2.0) = 12.5$
$(x - 15) / (3.8 - 2.0) = 12.5$, so $x = 37.5$
$37.5 - 35 = 2.5$

29. **(D)**   The Fortran course **decreased** from 100 students to 75 students. The Pascal course **decreased** from 175 students to 125 students. The Basic course **increased** from 100 students to 137 students, and

$$137 - 100 = 37$$

student increase. The COBOL course **increased** from 25 students to 87 students, and

$$87 - 25 = 62$$

student increase.

Answer (A) is wrong because the number decreased from 100 to 75 students.

$$75 - 100 = -25 < 62$$

Answer (B) is wrong because the number decreased from 175 to 125 students.

$$125 - 175 = -50 < 62$$

Answer (C) is wrong because the increase in students was less than 62.

$$137 - 100 = 37 < 62$$

30. **(C)**   211, 926

The number of ways to get 3 diamonds is $_{13}C_3 = 286$.

$$_{39}C_3 = \frac{11 \times 12 \times 13}{3 \times 2 \times 1} = 286$$

The remaining 2 cards must be chosen from the 39 cards which are <u>not</u> diamonds, and this can be done in

$$_{39}C_2 = \frac{39 \times 38}{2 \times 1} = 741$$

ways. Finally, $(286)(741) = 211,926$.

31. **(C)**

What percent of 85 is 17?

translates to   ↓   ↓   is means "="

　　?   × 85 = 17   of means "×"

Solving this equation for "?" we divide both sides by 85 as follows:

The 85 in both the numerator and denominator on the left side cancel, and we are left with

$$? = \frac{17}{85}$$

Writing $^{17}/_{85}$ as a percent and moving the decimal point two places to the right in the quotient and attaching the percent sign, we get:

$$.20 = 20\%$$

Answer choice (A) is incorrect due to a swap of numerator and denominator.

$$^{85}/_{17} = 5 \cong 5\%$$

Answer choice (B) is incorrect because multiplication was used instead of division.

$$85 \times 17 = 1{,}445 \cong 14^9/_{20}\%$$

Answer choice (D) is incorrect because division and not subtraction should be used.

32. **(B)**

625 square feet $\times$ .30 room for Baby Grand Piano = 187.5 square feet

187.5 square feet for Baby Grand Piano + 46.7 square feet for stage

$$= 234.2 \text{ square feet}$$

Answer (A) is wrong because addition was incorrectly used.

$$30 + 46.7 = 76.7 \text{ square feet}$$

Answer (C) is wrong because of incorrect usage of a subtraction step.

$$625 - 30 - 46.7 = 548.3 \text{ square feet}$$

Answer (D) is wrong because of incorrect multiplication followed by a subtraction step.

$$46.7 \times .30 = 14.01$$
$$625 - 14.01 = 610.99 \text{ square feet}$$

33. **(B)** If John contributes $2x$ to Charity A and $3x$ to Charity B, then his contributions to A and B will be in the ratio of 2 to 3. Then

$$2x + 3x = 2{,}500, \text{ or } x = 500.$$

Therefore, he should contribute $2(500) = \$1{,}000$ to Charity A.

34. **(A)**
When $g = 30$

$$C = 270g - 3g^2 \quad \text{becomes}$$

$$C = 270(30) - 3(30)^2 \quad \text{substituting } g = 30$$

$$C = 8,100 - 3(900) \quad \text{multiplying through}$$

$$C = 8,100 - 2,700$$

$$C = 5,400$$

The monthly commission in January is $5,400.
When $g = 40$

$$C = 270g - 3g^2 \quad \text{becomes}$$

$$C = 270(40) - 3(40)^2 \quad \text{substituting } g = 40$$

$$C = 10,800 - 3(1,600) \text{multiplying through}$$

$$C = 10,800 - 4,800$$

$$C = 6,000$$

The monthly commission in February is $6,000.

To determine the gain in Sam's commission from January to February, we consider:

$$\text{Gain in commission} = \text{Commission in February} - \text{Commission in January}$$

$$= \$6,000 - \$5,400$$

$$\text{Gain in commission} = \$600$$

Answer choice (B) is incorrect because it only consists of the January commission.

$$270(30) - 3(30^2) = \$5,400$$

Answer choice (C) is incorrect because it only accounts for the February commission.

$$270(40) - 3(40^2) = \$6,000$$

Answer choice (D) is incorrect because the two commissions were added together.

$$6000 + 5400 = \$11,400$$

35. Find the least common multiple of (11+1) and (19+1), i.e., 12 and 20. This would be 60 days. Counting 59 days from January 1st leads to March 1st.

Tim's pay per shift = (85)(12) = 1,020 dollars.

Then:

1020/20 = $51

36. Carol has the least ability, since she gets a greater number of points as she successfully makes each foul shot than either Adam or Brenda.

Brenda's point total for 22 foul shots = 23.

$23 = 5x - 2$.

Solving, $x = 5$.

Carol only has to make 5 foul shots.

(40)(.60) = 24 successful foul shots = 48 points for Adam (total points = 2(24)). Then $48 = x + 1$, so $x = 47$. Brenda has to make 47 foul shots.

Part IV

37. **(B)** The number 15 has two factors, besides itself and 1—namely, 3 and 5. Both of these factors are prime numbers. The number 13 is a prime, so has only one prime factor—namely, itself. For the number 18, the factors are 1, 2, 3, 6, 9, and 18. For the number 20, the factors are 1, 2, 4, 5, 10, and 20.

38. **(D)** When any point (x, y) is reflected over the x-axis, its new coordinates become $(x, -y)$. Thus A' will be located at $(2, -1)$ and B' will be located at $(1, -4)$. The slope of $\overline{A'B'} = [-4 - (-1)] / [1 - 2] = 3$.

39. **(C)** Since 2/5 of the students are men, 3/5 of the students must be women. We know that two-thirds of the women have blond hair, so $(2/3)(3/5) = 2/5$ of all the students are women with blond hair. This means $1/2 - 2/5 = 1/10$ of all the students are men with blond hair. Finally, $2/5 - 1/10 = 3/10$ of all the students are men who do NOT have blond hair.

40. **(A)** Since $m \angle P > 90°$, $QR^2 > PQ^2 + PR^2 = 8^2 + 10^2 = 164$. Then $QR > \sqrt{164}$, which is approximately 12.8. The minimum value of QR must be 13, since the lengths of all sides are integers. The minimum value of the perimeter is $8 + 10 + 13 = 31$.

41. **(C)** A total of $3{,}150/25 = 126$ teachers are in the school district currently. If the school enrollment increases by 20%, there will be $(3{,}150)(1.20) = 3{,}780$ students. In order to have a 1:18 teacher–student ratio, there must be $3{,}780/18 = 210$ teachers. Thus, the number of additional teachers needed is $210 - 126 = 84$.

42. **(B)** Note that $3^1 = 3$, $3^2 = 9$, $3^3 = 27$, $3^4 = 81$, $3^5 = 243$, etc. The pattern of the units digit is in blocks of 3, 9, 7, 1. These correspond to the consecutive powers of 3, beginning with 3^1. When 1,000,000 is divided by 3, the remainder is 1, so this corresponds to a units digit of 3.

43. **(B)** P (A or B, but not both) $= 1 - P(A \cap B) - P$ (Neither A nor B) $= 1 - (.60)(.30) - (.40)(.70) = .54$.

44. **(D)** To find the actual width (w) of this plot of land, use the proportion $14/8 = 224/w$. Solving, $w = 128$ ft. Then the area is $(224)(128) = 28{,}672$ square feet.

45. **(A)** $a_3 = (1)(2) = 2$, $a_4 = (2)(2) = 4$, $a_5 = (2)(4) = 8$, and $a_6 = (4)(8) = 32$.

46. **(D)** The final reduced price would be $(0.90)^5$, which is approximately 59% of the original price. Thus, the percent reduction is $100\% - 59\% = 41\%$.

47.

- First we need to find how many combinations of four numbers can be selected from 20 numbers. The number of combinations is given by $_{20}C_4 = 4{,}845$. Since each ticket costs 50 cents, the amount of money needed is $(4{,}845)(\$0.50) = \$2{,}422.50$.

- The number of winning combinations is $_6C_4 = 15$. (The machine picks six numbers, but your ticket contains only four numbers.) Since there are a total of 4,845 combinations, the required probability is $15/4{,}845 \approx .0031$.

- There are 14 numbers that the lottery machine will not choose. Since $_{14}C_4 = 1{,}001$, the required probability is $1{,}001/4{,}845 \approx .2066$.

48.

- James's tax will be $2 + (.006)($800 – $200) = $5.60.

- Marianne's tax will be $5 + (.012)($600 – $100) = $11.00.

- As a nonresident, Linda would owe an annual tax of [52][$5 + (.012)($1,000 – $100)] = $821.60. If she were a resident, Linda's annual tax would be [52][$2 + (.006)($1,000 - $200)] = $353.60. Thus, her annual savings is $821.60 - $353.60 = $468.00.

NEW JERSEY

HSPA

High School Proficiency Assessment in
Mathematics

Practice
Test 2

REFERENCE INFORMATION FOR THE HSPA

12 inches = 1 foot
3 feet = 1 yard
36 inches = 1 yard
5,280 feet = 1 mile
1,760 yards = 1 mile

100 centimeters = 1 meter
1000 meters = 1 kilometer

1000 milliliters (mL) =
    1 liter (L)

60 seconds = 1 minute
60 minutes = 1 hour
24 hours = 1 day
7 days = 1 week
52 weeks = 1 year

1000 watt hours =
    1 kilowatt hour

1000 milligrams = 1 gram
100 centigrams = 1 gram
10 grams = 1 dekagram
1000 grams = 1 kilogram

8 fluid ounces = 1 cup
2 cups = 1 pint
2 pints = 1 quart
4 quarts = 1 gallon

Rectangle

Area = lw
Perimeter = $2(l + w)$

Triangle

Area = $\frac{1}{2} bh$

Parallelogram

Area = bh

Pythagorean Formula

$c^2 = a^2 + b^2$

$\pi \approx 3.14$ or $\frac{22}{7}$

Circle

Area = πr^2
Circumference = $2\pi r$

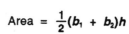

Trapezoid

Area = $\frac{1}{2}(b_1 + b_2)h$

Sphere

Volume = $\frac{4}{3}\pi r^3$

Cylinder

Volume = $\pi r^2 h$

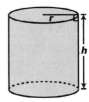

Rectangular Prism

Volume = lwh
Surface Area = $2lw + 2wh + 2lh$

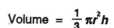

Cone

Volume = $\frac{1}{3}\pi r^2 h$

The sum of the measures of the interior angles of a triangle = 180°

The measure of a circle is 360° or 2π radians

Distance = rate * time   Interest = principal * rate * time

Compound Interest Formula: $A = p\left(1 + \frac{r}{k}\right)^{kt}$

A = amount after t years; p = principal; r = annual interest rate; t = number of years;

k = number of times compounded per year

The number of combinations of n elements taken r at a time is given by $\dfrac{n!}{(n-r)!r!}$

The number of permutations of n elements taken r at a time is given by $\dfrac{n!}{(n-r)!}$

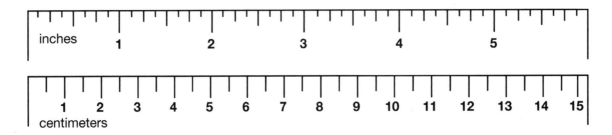

HSPA
Mathematics

Practice Test 2*
(See page 205 for answer sheets.)

TIME: 120 Minutes (Note: In the actual test administration, students will be given a brief break after each section.)
48 Questions

DIRECTIONS: Record your responses on the answer sheets provided.

Part I

1. $(-3 \times 10^{25}) \times (4 \times 10^{7}) =$

    (A) -12×10^{32} (C) -12×10^{18}

    (B) -12×10^{31} (D) 1×10^{32}

2. Solve for x.

    $5x - 2y = 20$

    $2x + 3y = 27$

    (A) $^{6}/_{19}$ (C) 5

    (B) $^{6}/_{11}$ (D) 6

3. An excavation for a building is 30 yards long, 10 yards wide, and $20^{1}/_{2}$ yards deep. If a cubic yard of earth weighs approximately 9 pounds, what will the weight of the earth (that fills the excavation) be when the excavation is filled to the top?

    (A) 270 pounds   (C) 2,700 pounds

    (B) $683^{1}/_{3}$ pounds   (D) 55,350 pounds

4. The first four terms of a sequence are

    $1, 4, 9, 16, \ldots$

    Assuming the pattern continues, what is the sum of the fifth and sixth terms?

---

* **The HSPA test is given over a two- or three-day period. Testing times and section lengths are approximate, and will vary from administration to administration.**

(A) 11   (C) 61

(B) 36   (D) 91

5. Answer the question based on the following diagram.

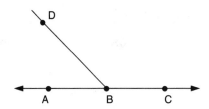

If segment $\overline{DB}$ meets line AC at point B, which of the following is true?

(A) $\angle ABD$ and $\angle DBC$ are supplementary angles.

(B) Segment $\overline{DB}$ is perpendicular to line AC.

(C) $\angle ABD$ and $\angle DBC$ are complementary angles.

(D) $\angle ABD$ and $\angle DBC$ are vertical angles.

6. A car salesperson receives $575 a week in addition to 3% commission on all cars whose sticker price is above $4,500. One week he sold a Ford for $8,785 and a Buick for $5,832. How much did he earn that week?

(A) $749.96   (C) $1,013.51

(B) $838.55   (D) $4,385.10

7. Read the graph, then answer the question.

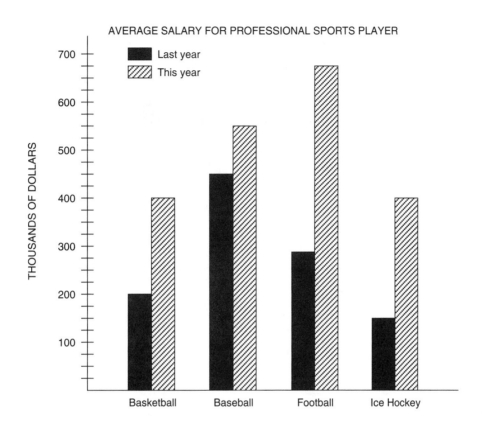

AVERAGE SALARY FOR PROFESSIONAL SPORTS PLAYER

Which sport showed the greatest increase in average salary between last year and this year?

(A) Basketball

(C) Football

(B) Baseball

(D) Ice Hockey

8. John ran three laps around his school track. John's coach wrote the following notes describing John's performance.

1) First time around – took 5 minutes.

2) Second time around – took 20% longer than first time around.

3) Third time around – took 30% longer than second time around.

What was John's total running time for the three laps?

(A) 17.5 min.

(C) 19.2 min.

(B) 18.8 min.

(D) 20.3 min.

9. If $-\frac{1}{7}x - 6 = 34$, find the value of $-2x + 3$.

   (A) -280 (C) 395

   (B) -77 (D) 563

10. If a couple getting married today can be expected to have 0, 1, 2, 3, 4, or 5 children with probabilities of 20%, 20%, 30%, 20%, 8%, and 2%, respectively, what is the average number of children, to the nearest tenth, couples getting married today have?

    (A) 1.0   (C) 2.0

    (B) 1.8   (D) 2.2

11. A botanist found that a certain forest contains only pine, spruce, oak, and maple trees. These trees appear in a ratio of approximately 3:2:4:5, respectively. Out of 1,000 trees in this forest, how many would be expected to be oaks?

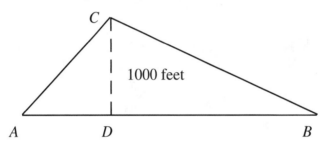

12. In this diagram, one person is standing at point A, one person is at point B, and both are looking at a helicopter at point C. The helicopter is 1000 feet above the ground on which the two people are standing.

    - If the angle of elevation at point A is 60° and the angle of elevation at point B is 20°, approximately how many feet apart are A and B?

    - How much further is the distance from B to the helicopter than from A to the helicopter?

Part II

13. Which sum is the greatest?

    (A) $1^2 + 1^3 + 1^4$ (C) $1^8 + 1^9 + 1^{10}$

    (B) $1^5 + 1^6 + 1^7$ (D) They are all equal.

14. Consider the sequence

    $$\frac{x}{x^2}, \frac{x^2}{x^3}, \frac{x^3}{x^4}, \frac{x^4}{x^5}, \dots$$

    where x is not allowed to equal zero. Each successive term of this sequence is

    (A) larger than the previous term.

    (B) smaller than the previous term.

    (C) equal to the previous term.

    (D) the relationship cannot be determined without knowing the value of x.

15. Read the graph, then answer the question.

    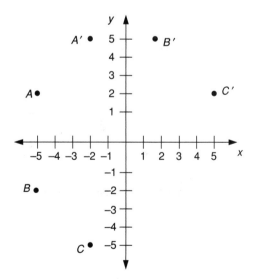

    If you plot the reflections of the given points about the line $y = -x$, then what would the radius of the circle that contains all the points be?

(A) 5   (C) 29

(B) $\sqrt{29}$ (D) 59

Question 16 refers to the following diagram. All lines are parallel or perpendicular.

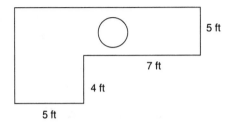

16. George must paint his bedroom ceiling. The diagram above represents his bedroom and includes a circular light fixture with a diameter of 2 feet. A gallon of paint covers 16 square feet and costs $8.95. How much will George have to spend on paint to cover the entire ceiling except for the light fixture? Assume he cannot buy a fraction of a gallon of paint.

(A) $35.80   (C) $44.75

(B) $42.99   (D) $50.20

17. Answer the question based on the following diagram.

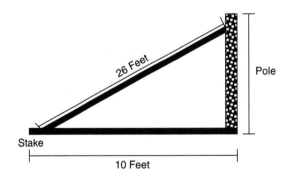

A 26-foot wire reaches from the top of a pole to a stake in the ground. If the distance from the base of the pole to the stake is 10 feet, how high is the pole?

(A) 6 feet   (C) $2\sqrt{65}$ feet

(B) 16 feet   (D) 24 feet

18. A bag contains 6 white balls, 3 red balls, and one blue ball. If one ball is drawn from the bag, what is the probability it will be white?

    (A) 0.1   (C) $0.3\overline{3}$

    (B) 0.3   (D) 0.6

19. What is the measure of the angle made by the minute and hour hand of a clock at 3:30?

    (A) 60°   (C) 90°

    (B) 75°   (D) 115°

20. What is the least prime number which is a divisor of $7^9 + 11^{25}$?

    (A) 1   (C) 3

    (B) 2   (D) $7^9 + 11^{25}$

21. A well-balanced coin is flipped 10,000 times. What is the probability of getting more than 5,100 heads?

    (A) 2.01%   (C) 2.28%

    (B) 2.22%   (D) 42.17%

22. John was looking for the smallest wrench in his tool box. If he has four wrenches, and the sizes are $^1/_2$ inch, $^3/_8$ inch, $^7/_8$ inch, and $^9/_{16}$ inch, which is the smallest?

    (A) $\dfrac{3}{8}$ in.   (C) $\dfrac{9}{16}$ in.

    (B) $\dfrac{1}{2}$ in.   (D) $\dfrac{7}{8}$ in.

23. Consider the following chart with 4 columns and 50 rows.

	Column A	Column B	Column C	Column D
Row 1	1	300	1	6
Row 2	8	297	4	17
Row 3	15	294	9	39
Row 4	22	291	16	83
Row 5	29	288	25	171
...	...	...	...	...
Row 50	?	?	?	?

- Assuming columns A and B are linear (but NOT C and D), find the numbers for columns A, B and C for row 50.

- In which column would the number 256 be found? Explain.

- What is the entry for the 30th row of column A?

- In what row will the number 1403 appear in column D?

24. What is the area, in square feet, of the triangular region in the diagram shown here?

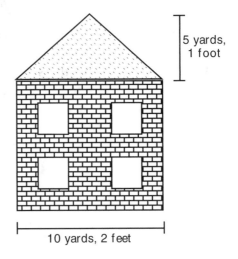

5 yards, 1 foot

10 yards, 2 feet

Part III

25. In a school building there are 10 rooms having fire escapes for every 20 rooms total. If the school building has a total of 150 rooms, how many rooms have fire escapes?

    (A) 75   (C) 135

    (B) 80   (D) 140

26. Read the graph, then answer the question.

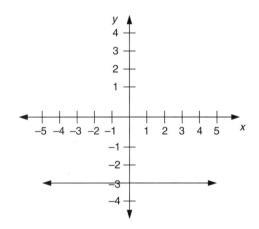

    Which equation is represented above?

    (A) $y = 3$ (C) $x = 3$

    (B) $y = -3$ (D) $x = -3$

27. Examine the pattern sequence and answer the question below.

    284   280   140   136   68   64   32   ___

    What number is missing in the sequence?

    (A) 8   (C) 28

    (B) 16   (D) 30

28. A gardener wishes to decorate a garden which is 576 square feet in area, and he must decide how to apportion each section of the garden

with specific plants. He has decided to set aside 20% of the garden with roses and an additional 32.9 square feet for a tomato patch. How much of the garden is set aside for the roses and tomatoes?

(A) 52.9 square feet

(C) 523.1 square feet

(B) 148.1 square feet

(D) 569.42 square feet

29. Read the graph below, then answer the question.

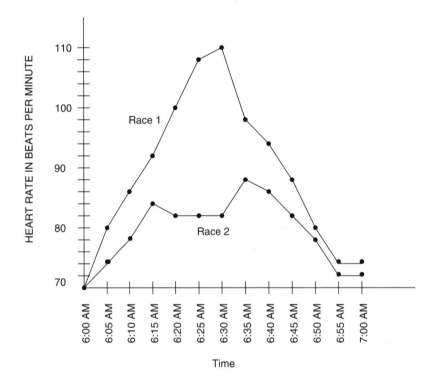

A runner has her heartbeat recorded for two 10.1-mile races run in the same park near her home, held on different days, and both starting at 6 AM.

Which of the following is true at 6:20 AM for the recorded heart rates for Race #1 and Race #2?

(A) Both recorded heart rates are increasing.

(B) Both recorded heart rates are decreasing.

(C) The recorded heart rate for Race #1 is increasing, and the recorded heart rate for Race #2 is stable.

(D) The recorded heart rate for Race #1 is stable, and the recorded heart rate for Race #2 is increasing.

30. Which two points would connect to give the slope whose absolute value is lowest?

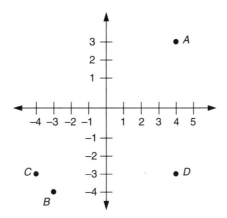

(A) $\overline{AD}$ (C) $\overline{BC}$

(B) $\overline{BD}$ (D) $\overline{CD}$

31. 23% of 460 is what?

(A) 10.58   (C) 105.8

(B) 20   (D) 2,000

32. In 23 years, John will be five times as old as he is today. If R = John's age in 23 years, which of the following equations could be used to determine John's age in 23 years?

(A) $5R - 23 = R$ (C) $5R - 115 = R$

(B) $\dfrac{R}{5} = 23$ (D) $5R = 23$

33. An owner of a delicatessen is thinking of constructing a parking lot in back of his store. He would like to have 35 parking spaces, and will need 2 pounds of cement for each parking space. If he buys 40 more pounds of cement than he expects to use, how many pounds of cement does he buy?

    (A) 30 pounds

    (B) 70 pounds

    (C) 110 pounds

    (D) 1,470 pounds

For the next two questions:

In this game, each player has red and black chips. Both players place on the table, simultaneously, a single chip. For the chart shown, a positive number means a gain for Player 1 (and thus a loss for Player 2). A negative number indicates a loss for player 1 (and thus a gain for Player 2). R=Red, B=Black.

Player 2

		R	B
Player 1	R	+$3	−$4
	B	−$1	+$1

34. Suppose Player 1 is conservative, and Player 2 wants to minimize Player 1's gains. How should each player play?

    (A) Player 1 plays red and Player 2 plays black.

    (B) Player 1 plays black and Player 2 plays red.

    (C) Both players play red.

    (D) Both players play black.

35. Suppose Player 1 adopts the strategy to alternate colors, beginning with red. If Player 2 has figured out Player 1's strategy, what is the expected loss for Player 1? Explain.

36. A probability experiment consists of first tossing a 5-sided die followed by tossing an 8-sided die. Assume the 5-sided die is numbered 1 through 5 and the 8-sided die is numbered 1 through 8. Let event A represent getting a higher number on the second die than on the first die. Let event B represent getting a sum of 10 from both dice.

    • Write the outcomes of each event.

    • Write the outcomes of A ∩ B.

    • What is the probability of the event A ∪ B?

Part IV

37. The graph below represents the high temperature for five days of the week. Which day has the greatest increase in temperature over that of the previous day?

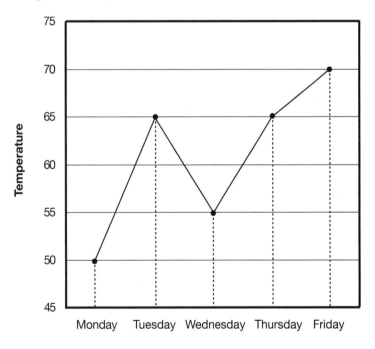

    (A) Tuesday   (C) Thursday

    (B) Wednesday   (D) Friday

38. The graph below shows the average monthly rainfall for the city of Batesville. During the month that had the third-smallest amount of rainfall, how many inches did it rain?

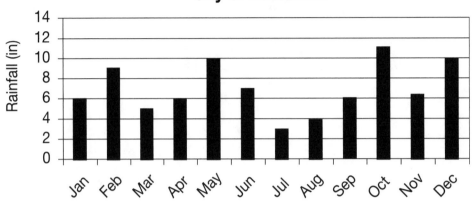

Average Monthly Rainfall for the City of Batesville

(A) 3   (C) 5

(B) 4   (D) 6

39.

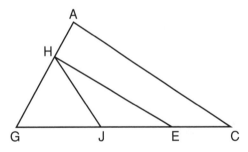

Note: The figure is not drawn to scale.

Given HG = HJ = JE, $\overline{HE}$ is parallel to $\overline{AC}$ and $m\angle AHJ = 128°$, what is $m\angle C$?

(A) 32°   (C) 52°

(B) 44°   (D) 64°

40. Two cylinders have the same volume. If the radius of cylinder I is 3 times the radius of cylinder II, then the height of cylinder II is how many times the height of cylinder I?

(A) 12   (C) 6

(B) 9   (D) 3

41. Which of the following triangles $A'B'C'$ is the image of $\triangle ABC$ that results from reflecting $\triangle ABC$ across the y-axis?

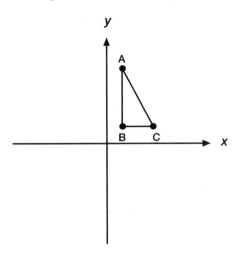

(A)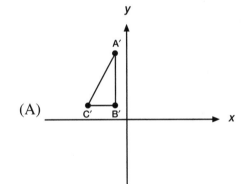

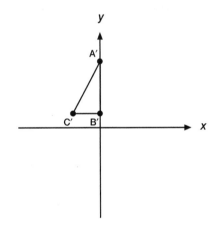

(C)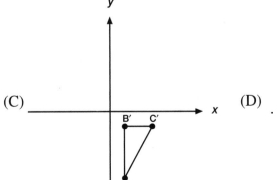

(D)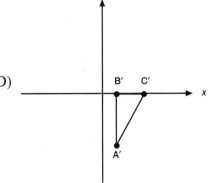

42. What is the 422nd digit to the right of the decimal point for the number $0.5\overline{3142}$?

    (A) 1   (C) 3

    (B) 2   (D) 4

43. On the *xy*-coordinate plane, point O is the origin. Suppose vector $\overrightarrow{\mathbf{OE}} = (3, 8)$ and vector $\overrightarrow{\mathbf{OF}} = (-2, -4)$. What ordered pair represents vector $\overrightarrow{\mathbf{EF}}$?

    (A) (–12, –5)   (C) (4, 1)

    (B) (–5, –12)   (D) (1, 4)

44. An item in a store will be marked up 30% tomorrow, and then will be discounted 40% from tomorrow's price the day after tomorrow. If the storeowner wants to apply one single discount equivalent to these two changes, what percent discount would that be?

    (A) 10   (C) 18

    (B) 14   (D) 22

45. A dartboard consists of a circle inside a rectangle, as shown below.

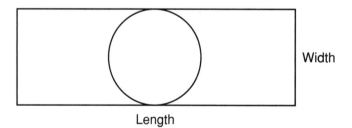

Length

The diameter of the circle equals the width of the rectangle. If the length of the rectangle is 20 units and its area is 160 square units, what is the approximate probability that a dart that lands inside the rectangle will also land inside the circle?

    (A) .05   (C) .25

    (B) .13   (D) .31

46.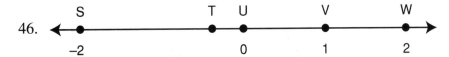

On the number line shown above, where would you find the point that corresponds to the quotient of the coordinate of W divided by the coordinate of T? (Note that the actual coordinate of T is not shown.)

(A) Between points V and W (C) Between points S and U

(B) Between points U and V (D) To the left of point S

47. Every weekend, Phil drives from his home to his favorite amusement park, a distance of 60 miles.

- If he averages 40 miles per hour for the first half of the trip, what must be his average speed for the second half of the trip in order for him to average 50 miles per hour for the entire trip?

- Suppose that on the trip home, Phil decides to stop for a 30-minute dinner break. If he averages 45 miles per hour for the first half of this return trip and 60 miles per hour for the second half of this trip, how many more MINUTES will the return trip take compared with the trip going to the park? (Be sure to account for his dinner break.)

48. Each weekend, a radio station gives away a free concert ticket to every 75th caller and a free CD to every 20th caller.

- If a total of 190 people called last weekend, how many people received a free concert ticket, and how many received a free CD?

- How many additional callers would have been needed for a person to receive both a free concert ticket and a free CD?

- If the radio station had decided to give away to every 8th caller a free dinner to a fancy restaurant, in addition to the concert tickets and CDs, how many of the first 100 callers would have received both a free CD and a free dinner? Also, what numbered caller(s) would be the winner(s) of both?

HSPA
PRACTICE TEST 2

ANSWER KEY

MATHEMATICS

Part I

1.	(A)	5.	(A)	9.	(D)
2.	(D)	6.	(C)	10.	(B)
3.	(D)	7.	(C)	11.	Open-Ended
4.	(C)	8.	(B)	12.	Open-Ended

Part II

13.	(D)	17.	(D)	21.	(C)
14.	(C)	18.	(D)	22.	(A)
15.	(B)	19.	(B)	23.	Open-Ended
16.	(C)	20.	(B)	24.	Open-Ended

Part III

25.	(A)	29.	(C)	33.	(C)
26.	(B)	30.	(D)	34.	(D)
27.	(C)	31.	(C)	35.	Open-Ended
28.	(B)	32.	(C)	36.	Open-Ended

Part IV

37.	(A)	41.	(A)	45.	(D)
38.	(C)	42.	(C)	46.	(D)
39.	(A)	43.	(B)	47.	Open-Ended
40.	(B)	44.	(D)	48.	Open-Ended

DETAILED EXPLANATIONS OF ANSWERS

TEST 2

Part I

1. **(A)**

$$(-3 \times 10^{25}) \times (4 \times 10^7) = (-3 \times 4) \times (10^{25} \times 10^7)$$
$$= -12 \times 10^{25+7}$$

In multiplication of terms with the same base, we add exponents.

$$= -12 \times 10^{32}$$

Answer choice (B) is incorrect because the exponents are improperly added.

$$(-3 \times 10^{25}) \times (4 \times 10^7) = (-3 \times 4) \times 10^{25+7} = -12 \times 10^{31}$$

Answer choice (C) is incorrect because the exponents should be added, **not** subtracted.

$$(-3 \times 10^{25}) \times (4 \times 10^7) = (-3 \times 4) \times 10^{25-7} = -12 \times 10^{18}$$

Answer choice (D) is incorrect because 4 and -3 should be multiplied, **not** added.

$$(-3 \times 10^{25}) \times (4 \times 10^7) = (4 + (-3)) \times 10^{25+7} = 1 \times 10^{32}$$

2. **(D)**

$$5x - 2y = 20$$
$$2x + 3y = 27$$

Multiply the bottom equation by 2 and the top equation by 3, so that the terms in the y-column will cancel as follows (if the y-terms cancel, you will be solving for x):

$$3(5x - 2y) = 3(20) \qquad 15x - 6y = 60$$
$$2(2x + 3y) = 2(27) \quad \Rightarrow \quad 4x + 6y = 54$$
$$19x = 114$$
$$19 \qquad\qquad 19$$
$$x = 6$$

Add the coefficients/terms in the *x*-column and the constants on the right side. Then divide both sides by 19, the coefficient of the *x*-term.

Answer choice (A) is incorrect because it solves the equation incorrectly.

$$15x - 6y = 60$$
$$4x + 6y = 54$$
$$19x = 6$$
$$x = {}^6/_{19}$$

Answer choice (B) is incorrect because it assumes errors in signs.

$$15x - 6y = 60$$
$$4x + 6y = 54$$
$$11x = 6$$
$$x = {}^6/_{11}$$

Answer choice (C) is incorrect because it solves for *y*.

$$2(5x - 2y = 20) = 10x - 4y = 40$$
$$5(2x + 3y = 27) = -(10x + 15y = 135)$$
$$-19y = -95$$
$$y = 5$$

3. **(D)**
    The volume of the rectangular excavation for the building

    = (length) (width) (height)

    = (30) (10) (20$^1/_2$)

    = (300) (20$^1/_2$)

    $$= \frac{300}{1} \times \frac{41}{2} = \frac{150}{1} \times \frac{41}{1}$$

    (writing quantities in fractional form)

    = 6,150 cubic yards,

cancelling and multiplying numerators.

If a cubic yard of earth weighs approximately 9 pounds and there are

6,150 cubic yards in the excavation, the weight of the earth that fills the space produced by the excavation is

(6,150 ~~cubic yards~~) (9 pounds/~~cubic yard~~) = 55,350 pounds

when the excavation is filled with earth.

Answer choice (A) is incorrect because it deletes the width and height from the computation.

30 yards × 9 pounds/cubic yard = 270 pounds

Answer choice (B) is incorrect because it divides by the weight per volume.

$(30 \times 10 \times 20\frac{1}{2}) \div 9$ pounds/cubic yard = $683\frac{1}{3}$

Answer choice (C) is incorrect because it deletes the height from the computation.

(30 yards × 10 yards) × 9 pounds/cubic yard = 2,700 pounds

4. **(C)** Each term of the sequence is a perfect square.

1, 4, 9, 16, …

$= 1^2, 2^2, 3^2, 4^2, \ldots$

The fifth term will be 5^2, or 25.

The sixth term will be 6^2, or 36.

The sum of the fifth and sixth terms is 25 + 36 = 61.

The answer is (C).

5. **(A)** $\angle ABC$ is a straight angle. The number of degrees in a straight angle is 180°. When the sum of two angles is 180°, the angles are said to be supplementary. In the diagram

$\angle ABD + \angle DBC = \angle ABC$. Therefore,

$\angle ABD + \angle DBC = 180°$

and $\angle ABD$ and $\angle DBC$ are supplementary angles.

Answer choice (B) is incorrect because it assumes

$\angle ABD = \angle DBC = 90°$

Answer choice (C) is incorrect because it assumes

$$\angle ABD + \angle DBC = 90°$$

Answer choice (D) is incorrect because $\angle ABD$ and $\angle DBC$ are adjacent angles, not vertical angles.

6. **(C)**

The salary for the week

$$= \$575 + .03 \text{ (cars sold above \$4,500)}$$

$$= \$575 + .03 \ (\$8,785 + \$5,832)$$

$$= \$575 + .03(\$14,617)$$

$$= \$575 + \$438.51$$

$$= \$1,013.51$$

We add the sales of $8,785 + $5,832, which are prices of cars sold above $4,500, change 3% to .03 and multiply .03 ($14,617) first, by order of operations before adding on the $575.

Answer choice (A) is incorrect because it takes 3% of $5,832 only and adds this to her base pay.

$$\$5,832 \times .03 = \$174.96 + \$575 = \$749.96$$

Answer choice (B) is incorrect because it takes 3% of $8,785 only and adds this to her base pay.

$$\$8,785 \times .03 = \$263.55 + \$575 = \$838.55$$

Answer choice (D) is incorrect because it takes 3% of $14,617 incorrectly.

$$.03 \times \$14,617 = \$438.51 = \$4,385.10$$

7. **(C)** The average salary for basketball players increased from

$200,000 to $400,000

and $400,000 − $200,000 = $200,000 increase

The average salary for baseball players increased from

$450,000 to $550,000

and $550,000 − $450,000 = $100,000 increase

The average salary for football players increased from

$300,000 to $675,000

and $675,000 – $300,000 = $375,000 increase

The average salary for ice hockey players increased from

$150,000 to $400,000

and $400,000 – $150,000 = $250,000 increase

Football players' salaries increased by $375,000, which is the highest increase. Therefore, (A), (B), and (D) are incorrect.

8.   **(B)**   We need to find the running time for each of the three laps.

Time for the first lap = 5 min.   (given in the problem)

Time for the second lap = time for the first lap
                            + 20% of time for the first lap

= 5 min. + (.20 × 5 min.)

= 5 min. + 1 min.

= 6 min.

Time for the third lap = time for the second lap
                            + 30% of time for the second lap

= 6 min. + (.30 × 6 min.)

= 6 min. + 1.8 min.

= 7.8 min.

The total running time can now be found by adding together the times for each of the three laps.

Total time = 5 min. + 6 min. + 7.8 min.

= 18.8 min.

The answer is (B).

9.   **(D)**
To solve for x in:

$$-\tfrac{1}{7}x - 6 = 34$$

$$+6 \quad +6$$

$$-\tfrac{1}{7}x \quad = 40$$

Add +6 to both sides; since the x term is on the left side, we transpose the constant term (–6) on the left side to the right side.

Then continue to solve for x in $-1/_7 x = 40$ by multiplying both sides of the equation by (–7). In this way the 7's on the left side will cancel to yield the result.

$$-1/_7 x = 40$$

$$(-7)(-1/_7)x = (-7)(40)$$

$$x = -280$$

Now continue to substitute $x = -280$ in the expression $-2x + 3$ as follows:

$$-2(-280) + 3 =$$

$$560 + 3 = 563$$

Answer choice (A) is incorrect because –280 is the value of x, not the value of the expression $-2x + 3$. Answer choice (B) is incorrect because it supposes an incorrect value for x.

$$-1/_7 x - 6 = 34$$

$$+6 \quad +6$$

$$-1/_7 x = 40 \quad \text{(Step 1)}$$

Then $-2x + 3 = -2(40) + 3 = -80 + 3 = -77$

Answer choice (C) is incorrect because it reveals an error in solving for x:

$$-1/_7 x - 6 = 34$$

$$-6 \quad -6$$

$$-1/_7 x \quad = 28$$

$$x = -196 \quad \text{(Step 1)}$$

Then Step 2 takes $x = -196$ and substitutes it in the expression

$$-2x + 3 =$$

$$-2(-196) + 3 =$$

$$392 + 3 = 395 \quad \text{(Step 2)}$$

10. **(B)**   Average number of children equals the sum of the products of each separate value and its corresponding probability. Thus, the average number of children = (0) (.20) + (1) (.20) + (2) (.30) + (3) (.20) + (4) (.08) + (5) (.02) = 0 + .20 + .60 + .60 +.32 + .10 = 1.82. So, choice B is the best approximation.

11.   It is important to be sure you understand the notation used in this problem. This notation 3:2:4:5 (for pine:spruce:oak:maple) is a compact way of expressing the following information:

3 pine trees:2 spruce trees:4 oak trees:5 maple trees

1)   For every three pine trees, there are two spruce trees, or the ratio of pine to spruce is $^3/_2$.

2)   For every three pine trees, there are four oak trees, or the ratio of pine to oak is $^3/_4$.

3)   For every three pine trees, there are five maple trees, or the ratio of pine to maple is $^3/_5$.

4)   For every two spruce trees, there are four oak trees, or the ratio of spruce to oak is $^2/_4$.

5)   For every two spruce trees, there are five maple trees, or the ratio of spruce to maple is $^2/_5$.

6)   For every four oak trees, there are five maple trees, or the ratio of oak to maple is $^4/_5$.

Look again at the numbers 3:2:4:5. If you add these numbers together, you get a total of

3 + 2 + 4 + 5 = 14.

Thus, out of every 14 trees,

3 are pine ($\dfrac{3}{14}$ of the trees are pine)

2 are spruce ($\dfrac{2}{14}$ of the trees are spruce)

4 are oak ($\dfrac{4}{14}$ of the trees are oak)

5 are maple ($\dfrac{5}{14}$ of the trees are maple)

(14 trees selected at random would probably not yield these ratios, but in a large sample, on average, the ratios will hold.)

Having found that $^4/_{14}$ of the trees are oaks, we can solve the problem by using a proportion.

$$\frac{4 \text{ oaks}}{14 \text{ trees}} = \frac{x \text{ oaks}}{1,000 \text{ trees}}$$

Cross-multiplying gives

$$(14)(x) = (4)(1,000)$$

Solving for x, we find

$$x = \frac{(4)(1,000)}{14}$$

$$= 285.7 \text{ oaks}$$

Since the number of trees must be a whole number, this answer is rounded to

$$x = 286 \text{ oaks.}$$

12. Let x = distance from A to D. Tan 60° = 1000/x, so x = 577.35 feet. Let y = distance from D to B. Tan 20° = 1000/y, so y = 2747.48 feet. Thus, x + y ≈ 3325 feet.

$$AC = \sqrt{577.35^2 + 1000^2} \approx 1154.7 \text{ feet}$$

$$BC = \sqrt{2747.48^2 + 1000^2} \approx 2923.8 \text{ feet}$$

$$BC - AC \approx 1769 \text{ feet}$$

Part II

13. **(D)**   To solve this problem, you only need to remember one important fact: 1 raised to any power will always equal 1.

Using this fact, we see that the expressions in parts (A), (B), and (C) are equal. They can be re-written as 1 + 1 + 1, which equals 3.

The answer is (D).

14. **(C)**   We can simplify each term by cancelling x's from the numerator and denominator.

$$\text{First term} = \frac{x}{x^2} = \frac{x}{x \times x} = \frac{1}{x}$$

(Cancelled one x from the numerator with one x from the denominator.)

$$\text{Second term} = \frac{x^2}{x^3} = \frac{x \times x}{x \times x \times x} = \frac{1}{x}$$

(Cancelled two x's from the numerator with two x's from the denominator.)

$$\text{Third term} = \frac{x^3}{x^4} = \frac{x \times x \times x}{x \times x \times x \times x} = \frac{1}{x}$$

(Cancelled three x's from the numerator with three x's from the denominator.)

$$\text{Fourth term} = \frac{x^4}{x^5} = \frac{x \times x \times x \times x}{x \times x \times x \times x \times x} = \frac{1}{x}$$

(Cancelled four x's from the numerator with four x's from the denominator.)

Since there is always one more x in the denominator than in the numerator, all terms in this sequence equal $1/x$. Thus, each term is equal to the previous term, regardless of the value of x.

The same result can also be obtained by using the following law of exponents:

$$\frac{x^a}{x^b} = x^{a-b}$$

Applying this law gives

$$\text{First term} \quad = \frac{x}{x^2} = x^{1-2} \quad = x^{-1}$$

$$\text{Second term} \quad = \frac{x^2}{x^3} = x^{2-3} \quad = x^{-1}$$

$$\text{Third term} \quad = \frac{x^3}{x^4} = x^{3-4} \quad = x^{-1}$$

$$\text{Fourth term} \quad = \frac{x^4}{x^5} = x^{4-5} = x^{-1}$$

Again we see that all the terms are equal. (Note that $x^{-1} = 1/x$, so either

approach to this problem yields the same result.)
   The answer is (C).

15. **(B)**

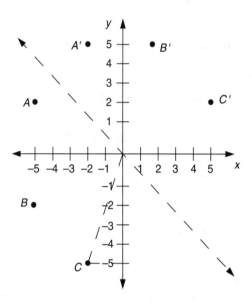

   As you can see, when you plot the reflections of *A*, *B*, and *C*, the resulting circle is centered on the origin. Hence, *C* and *B′* and *B* and *C′* would be endpoints of diameters. Since you know the center, by using the Pythagorean theorem or the distance formula (which is a variation of the Pythagorean theorem) and the coordinates of any of the points, you can determine the radius. Therefore, using point *C* it becomes

Pythagorean theorem   or   distance formula

$$a^2 + b^2 = c^2$$

$$\sqrt{a^2 + b^2} = c$$

$$\sqrt{(-5)^2 + (-2)^2} = c$$

$$\sqrt{29} = c$$

$$d = \sqrt{(x_2 - x_1)^2 + (y_2 - y_1)^2}$$

$$d = \sqrt{(-2 - 0)^2 + (-5 - 0)^2}$$

$$d = \sqrt{(-2)^2 + (-5)^2}$$

$$d = \sqrt{29}$$

16. **(C)** In order to solve this problem, we must determine the area of the ceiling. This is accomplished by drawing a line that creates two rectangles as shown in the accompanying figure.

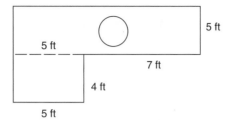

Determine the area of both rectangles using the formula

$A = \text{length} \times \text{width}$

The smaller rectangle will have an area of 5×4 or 20 sq. ft.

To find the length of the larger rectangle, use the information provided on the diagram. The lengths given on the bottom of the diagram are 7 and 5 which add up to 12.

Use the area formula and multiply 12 by 5, yielding 60 sq. ft.

Add the two areas together to obtain $60 + 20 = 80$.

Do not forget about the area of the light fixture. George does not want to paint over the fixture, so we must subtract the area of the light fixture from the total area of the ceiling.

The area of a circle is determined by the formula π times the radius squared.

We are given the diameter of the circle, 2 feet. The radius is half of the diameter, so our radius is 1 foot. Squaring this number leaves us with 1 still. So our formula is now π times 1. This will give us π which is equivalent to about 3.14.

Subtract the area of the light from the total area.

$80 - 3.14 = 76.86$

Next, determine how many times 16 (the number of square feet one gallon of paint covers) divides into 76.86.

$76.86 \div 16 = 4.8.$

To determine the cost of the project, multiply the number of gallons it will take to paint the ceiling by the price per gallon, $8.95.

Since the number of gallons did not come out to an even number, we must round this number up because you cannot buy $^8/_{10}$ of a gallon.

4.8 rounds up to 5.

5 gallons $8.95 = $44.75

17. **(D)** The triangle in the diagram is a right triangle. If the triangle is a right triangle, the lengths of the sides satisfy the Pythagorean property,

namely $a^2 + b^2 = c^2$, where a and b are the lengths of the legs of the right triangle and c is the length of the hypotenuse.

Therefore, $a^2 + b^2 = c^2$ translates to

(length from stake to pole)^2 + (length of pole)^2 = (length of wire)^2

$$10^2 + b^2 = 26^2$$

$$100 + b^2 = 676 \text{ Solving for } b^2$$

$$\underline{-100 \qquad\qquad -100}$$

$$b^2 = 576$$

and $b^2 = 576$ means to take the positive square root of both sides. Doing so yields $b = 24$.

Answer choice (A) is incorrect because it incorrectly uses the Pythagorean property.

$$\sqrt{26 + 10} = 6$$

Answer choice (B) is incorrect because it incorrectly uses the Pythagorean property.

$$26 \text{ feet} - 10 \text{ feet} = 16 \text{ feet}$$

Answer choice (C) is incorrect because it incorrectly uses the Pythagorean property.

18. **(D)**   There are 10 balls in all and 6 of them are white. Hence, the probability of drawing a white ball is

$$\frac{6}{10} = 0.6$$

19. **(B)**   At 3:30 the hands of the clock will be as shown below. The angle has a measure of 75°.

20. **(B)**   Since 7^9 and 11^{25} are both odd numbers, their sum is even. Thus, 2 is a divisor of $7^9 + 11^{25}$. Also, 2 is the smallest (least) prime.

21. **(C)**   The mean, μ, of the Binomial Distribution is *np, where n =*

number of coin flips and p = probability of getting heads on a single flip of the coin. In this case, $n = 10,000$ and $p = .5$, so $\mu = (10,000)(.5) = 5000$. We also need to calculate the standard deviation, σ, which represents the dispersion of the data. $\sigma = \sqrt{npq}$, where $q = 1 - p$. Then $\sigma = \sqrt{(10,000)(.5)(.5)} = 50$.

The next step is to convert 5100 to a standard score, z, defined as: $z = (x - \mu)/\sigma$, where $x = 5100$. Then $z = (5100 - 5000)/50 = 2$.

Finally, since this is considered a Normal Distribution, we need to find the probability that a z score is greater than 2. From a chart on Normal Distribution, this probability is approximately .0228 or 2.28%. This is choice C.

22. **(A)** Choices (C) and (D) are each more than $^1/_2$. Choice (B) is $^1/_2$. Only choice (A) is less than $^1/_2$.

23. Column A: Each row is 7 more than the previous row.

Row 50 entry = $1 + (7)(49) = 344$

Column B: Each row decreases by 3.

Row 50 entry = $300 - (3)(49) = 153$

Column C: Each row is a perfect square.

Row 50 entry = $(50)^2 = 2500$

The number 256 equals 16^2, so it would be found in Column C.

The 30th row of Column A = $1 + (29)(7) = 204$.

Column D's entries are found by multiplying the previous row by 2, then adding 5. Row 6 = 347, row 7 = 699, row 8 = 1403.

24. We will use the formula for the area of a triangle,

$$A = \frac{1}{2} \times base \times height$$

$$= \frac{1}{2}bh$$

However, since we want the final answer in square *feet*, we must first convert the given dimensions of the base and height from a combination of yards and feet into feet only. In order to make this conversion, we will use the fact that there are 3 feet in one yard.

For the base:

Multiply the number of yards in the base, 10 yards, by the conversion factor (3 feet/1 yard).

$$(10 \text{ yards}) \frac{3 \text{ feet}}{1 \text{ yard}} = 30 \text{ feet}$$

Notice that the word "yards" in the numerator cancels the word "yard" in the denominator (mathematically, it doesn't matter that one word is singular and one is plural); this cancellation of yards yields an answer in feet as desired.

We have just found that 10 yards = 30 feet. Thus,

$$\text{base} = 10 \text{ yards} + 2 \text{ feet} \qquad \text{(given)}$$
$$= 30 \text{ feet} + 2 \text{ feet} \qquad \text{(converted to ft.)}$$
$$= 32 \text{ feet}$$

For the height:

$$(5 \text{ yards}) \frac{3 \text{ feet}}{1 \text{ yard}} = 15 \text{ feet}$$

Thus,

$$\text{height} = 5 \text{ yards} + 1 \text{ foot} \qquad \text{(given)}$$
$$= 15 \text{ feet} + 1 \text{ foot} \qquad \text{(converted to ft.)}$$
$$= 16 \text{ feet}$$

Now we use the formula for the area of the triangle.

$$A = \frac{1}{2}bh$$
$$= \left(\frac{1}{2}\right)(32 \text{ ft.})(16 \text{ ft.})$$
$$= 256 \text{ ft}^2.$$

Part III

25. **(A)**

$$\frac{10 \text{ rooms total having fire escapes}}{20 \text{ rooms}} = \frac{?}{150 \text{ rooms}}$$

Solving this proportion for the "?"

$$? = \frac{10 \text{ rooms} \times 150 \text{ rooms}}{20 \text{ rooms}} = \frac{1,500 \text{ rooms}}{20 \text{ rooms}} = 75 \text{ rooms}$$

Answer choice (B) is incorrect because it shows

20 rooms – 10 rooms = 10 rooms with no fire escape

Assume   7 rooms/floor and 7 rooms/floor × 10 rooms = 70 rooms

and   150 rooms – 70 rooms = 80 rooms

Answer choice (C) is incorrect because it shows

20 rooms – (150 rooms ÷ 20 rooms) = 13.5 rooms

and   13.5 rooms × 10 rooms = 135 rooms

Answer choice (D) is incorrect because it shows

150 total rooms – (20 rooms – 10 rooms) = 140 rooms

26. **(B)**   The graph of $y = -3$ is parallel to the x-axis and passes through the point $(0, -3)$.

Answer choice (A) is incorrect because $y = 3$ represents the graph:

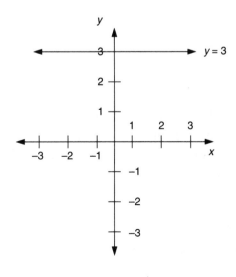

Answer choice (C) is incorrect because $x = 3$ represents the graph:

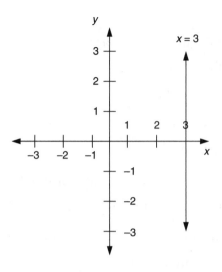

Answer choice (D) is incorrect because $x = -3$ represents the graph:

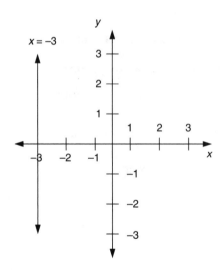

27. **(C)**   The second number is 4 less than the first. The third number is half the second. This pattern of subtracting 4 and then taking half of the resultant number continues, so the missing number should be $32 - 4$, or 28.

28. **(B)**

576 square feet $\times$ .20 garden for roses = 115.2 square feet

32.9 square feet for tomato patch + 115.2 square feet for roses

$$= 148.1 \text{ square feet}$$

Answer choice (A) is incorrect because it shows

$$20 \text{ square feet} + 32.9 \text{ square feet} = 52.9 \text{ square feet}$$

Answer choice (C) is incorrect because it shows

$$576 \text{ square feet} - 20 \text{ square feet} - 32.9 \text{ square feet} = 523.10 \text{ square feet}$$

Answer choice (D) is incorrect because it shows

$$32.9 \text{ square feet} \times .20 = 6.58 \text{ square feet}$$

and $576 - 6.58 = 569.42$ square feet

29. **(C)**   In the interval of 6:20 AM to 6:30 AM, one observes on the graph that for Race #1 the heart rate in beats per minute is increasing from 100 beats/minute to 110 beats/minute, as follows: (6:20, 100), (6:25, 108), (6:30, 110); while for Race #2 the heart rate in beats per minute is stable at 82 beats/minute, as follows: (6:20, 82), (6:25, 82), (6:30, 82).

Answer choice (A) is incorrect because the heart rate for Race #2 is steady. Answer choice (B) is incorrect because the heart rate for Race #1 is increasing, and the heart rate for Race #2 is steady. Answer choice (D) is incorrect because the answers are reversed: Race #2 is stable, and Race #1 is increasing.

30. **(D)**

$$M = \text{slope} = \frac{\Delta y}{\Delta x} = \frac{y_2 - y_1}{x_2 - x_1}$$

$$M_{AD} = \frac{-3 - 3}{4 - 4} = \emptyset \ \text{ undefined slope}$$

$$M_{BC} = \frac{-3 + 4}{-4 + 3} = -1 \quad |-1| = 1$$

$$M_{BD} = \frac{-3 + 4}{4 + 3} = \frac{1}{7}$$

$$M_{CD} = \frac{-3 + 3}{4 + 4} = 0$$

$$M_{AC} = \frac{-3 - 3}{-4 - 4} = \frac{6}{8} = \frac{3}{4}$$

$$M_{AB} = \frac{-4 - 3}{-3 - 4} = 1$$

Since zero is the lowest possible value, $\overline{CD}$ has the slope that is least steep.

31. **(C)**

$$23\% \quad \text{of} \quad 460 \quad \text{is} \quad \text{what?}$$

translates to $\quad \downarrow \quad \downarrow \quad \downarrow \quad \downarrow \quad \downarrow \qquad$ is means "="

$$.23 \quad \times \quad 460 \quad = \quad ? \qquad \text{of means "} \times \text{"}$$

and $23\% = .23$; to go from percent to decimal, drop the percent sign and move the decimal point two places to the left.

Solving this equation for "?" we multiply $.23 \times 460$ to get 105.8.

Answer choice (A) is incorrect because it shows

$$.23 \times 460 = .23 \times 46.0 = 10.58$$

Answer choice (B) is incorrect because it shows

$$\frac{460}{23} = 20.$$

Answer choice (D) is incorrect because it shows

$$\frac{460}{.23} = \frac{46{,}000}{23} = 2{,}000$$

32. **(C)**

$$R = \text{John's age in 23 years}$$

$$R - 23 = \text{John's age now}$$

$$5(R - 23) = \text{John's age in 23 years}$$

Then $\quad 5(R - 23) = R \Rightarrow 5R - 115 = R$

Choice (A) is incorrect because it shows wrong use of the distributive law. Choice (B) is incorrect because it asserts that "times" refers to division, not multiplication. Choice (D) is incorrect because the equation should be rewritten as $R + 23 = 5R$ when R represents John's age now.

33. **(C)**

2 pounds of cement/~~parking space~~ $\times$ 35 ~~parking spaces~~

$$= 70 \text{ pounds of cement}$$

70 pounds of cement + 40 extra pounds of cement

= 110 pounds of cement

Answer choice (A) is incorrect because it subtracts the 40 extra pounds of cement.

(2 pounds of cement/parking space × 35 parking spaces) – 40 pounds = 30 pounds

Answer choice (B) is incorrect because it does not add on the 40 extra pounds of cement.

2 pounds of cement/parking space × 35 parking spaces = 70 pounds

Answer choice (D) is incorrect because it shows

(40 pounds + 2 pounds) × 35 parking spaces = 1,470 pounds

34. **(D)** Both players play black. Since Player 1 is conservative, he does not want to risk a $4 loss, so he plays black. Player 2 is trying to minimize any gain for Player 1, so Player 2 will avoid playing red (since Player 1 could gain $3). Hence, Player 2 also plays black.

35. $2.50 is the expected loss for Player 1. Player 2 should alternate colors, beginning with black. Player 1's losses will appear as : $4, $1, $4, $1, $4, $1, etc. Over a long run, there will be as many $4 losses as $1 losses. Averaging $4 and $1 yields $2.50.

36. Outcomes for A: 1/2, 1/3, 1/4, 1/5, 1/6, 1/7, 1/8, 2/3, 2/4, 2/5, 2/6, 2/7, 2/8, 3/4, 3/5, 3/6, 3/7, 3/8, 4/5, 4/6, 4/7, 4/8, 5/6, 5/7, 5/8.

Outcomes for B: 2/8, 3/7, 4/6, 5/5.

Outcomes of A ∩ B: 2/8, 3/7, 4/6.

$P(A \cup B) = P(A) + P(B) - P(A \cap B) =$

$25/40 + 4/40 - 3/40 = 26/40 = 13/20$

Part IV

37. **(A)** Tuesday has the greatest increase in temperature over that of the previous day. The high temperature of Tuesday was 65, while for Monday it was 50. The difference is a 15-degree increase. On Wednesday, the temperature decreased 10 degrees. On Thursday, the temperature increased 10 degrees, and on Friday, the temperature increased only 5 degrees.

38. **(C)** The amount of rainfall is determined by looking at the length of the bars. First, find the shortest bar, which is July, and the second shortest, which is August. The third shortest is March. Next, looking left from March to the rainfall axis you can see that March had 5 inches of rain.

39. **(A)** $m \angle GHJ = 180° - m \angle AHJ = 52°$. $\triangle GHJ$ is isosceles, with $m \angle G = m \angle HJG = (180° - 52°)/2 = 64°$. Then $m \angle HJE = 180° - m \angle HJG = 116°$. $\triangle HJE$ is also isosceles, with $m \angle JHE = m \angle JEH = (180° - 116°)/2 = 32°$. Finally, since $\angle JEH$ and $\angle C$ are corresponding angles of parallel lines, $m \angle C = 32°$.

40. **(B)** The volume of a cylinder is given by the formula $V = \pi r^2 h$, where r is the radius and h is the height. Let x = the radius of cylinder II, so that $3x$ = the radius of cylinder I. If h_1 = the height of cylinder I and h_2 = the height of cylinder II, then the volume of cylinder I = $(\pi)(3x)^2(h_1) = 9\pi x^2 h_1$, and the volume of cylinder II = $\pi x^2 h_2$. Since the volumes are equal, $h_2 = 9h_1$.

41. **(A)** Find the y-axis. Find the side of the figure closest to the y-axis and measure the distance between this side and the y-axis. A reflection of the figure will put this side the same distance from the y-axis, but on the other side. Also, notice the point labeled C. A reflection of this point across the y-axis will also be the same distance from the y-axis, but on the other side.

42. **(C)** The repeating digits that follow the decimal point are initially in positions 2, 3, 4, 5. This means that the digit 3 will be found in positions 2, 6, 10, etc. The digit 1 will be found in positions 3, 7, 11, etc. The digit 4 will be found in positions 4, 8, 12, etc. The digit 2 will be found in positions 5, 9, 13, etc.

The best approach here is to divide 422 by 4, since there are 4 repeating digits. This will yield 105 with a remainder of 2. We need to find position numbers that, when divided by 4, also leave a remainder of 2. The position numbers corresponding to the digit 3 are the correct ones. Note that each of 2, 6, 10, etc., will yield a remainder of 2 when they are divided by 4.

43. **(B)**   The vector $\overrightarrow{\mathbf{EF}}$ is actually vector $\overrightarrow{\mathbf{OF}}$ – vector $\overrightarrow{\mathbf{OE}}$. The coordinates are found as $(-2 - [3], -4 - [8]) = (-5, -12)$.

44. **(D)**   For simplicity, assume that the item is initially $100. Tomorrow's price after the markup will be ($100)(1.30) = $130. The day after tomorrow, the price will be $130 – (.40)($130) = $78. A single discount of $22 would have had the same effect, and 22/100 = 22%.

45. **(D)**   Since the area of the rectangle is 160 square units, the width must be 160/20 = 8 units. This is also the diameter of the circle, so the radius = 4 units. The area of the circle = $(\pi)(4^2) = 16\pi$, which is approximately 50.27 square units. The required probability = $50.27/160 \approx .31$.

46. **(D)**   The coordinate of T is a negative number between –1 and 0, but closer to 0. Choose a potential value of T such as –.5. Then 2/–.5 = –4, which is located to the left of point S.

47. •   The time for the entire trip must be 60/50 = 1.2 hours. The time he has already used in traveling to the park is 30/40 = .75 hours. So, he must travel the remaining 30 miles in 1.2 –.75 = .45 hours. This means that his rate for the trip home must be 30/.45 $\approx$ 66.7 miles per hour.

  •   For the first part of the trip home, the time will be 30/45 = 2/3 hour. For the second part of the trip home, the time will be 30/60 = 1/2 hour. Adding the 1/2 hour for his dinner break, the total time will be 2/3 + 1/2 + 1/2 = 5/3 hour = 1 hour and 40 minutes. Since his trip to the park took 1.2 = 1 hour and 12 minutes, the additional time is 28 minutes.

48. •   190/75 = 2.53, so two people received a free concert ticket. Since 190/20 = 9.5, nine people received a free CD.

  •   In order for a person to receive both items, the number of the caller must be the least common multiple (LCM) of 75 and 20 (or a multiple of that number). The LCM of 75 and 20 is 300, so the additional number of callers needed is 300 – 190 = 110.

  •   The least common multiple of 8 and 20 is 40. A numbered caller—that is, any multiple of 40—would also be entitled to a free dinner and a free CD. The only multiples of 40 that are less than or equal to 100 are 40 and 80. Thus, the 40th and the 80th callers would receive both a free dinner and a free CD.

NEW JERSEY

HSPA

High School Proficiency Assessment in

Mathematics

ANSWER SHEETS

HSPA – Practice Test 1
Answer Sheet

Mathematics

1. (A) (B) (C) (D)   5. (A) (B) (C) (D)   9. (A) (B) (C) (D)
2. (A) (B) (C) (D)   6. (A) (B) (C) (D)   10. (A) (B) (C) (D)
3. (A) (B) (C) (D)   7. (A) (B) (C) (D)
4. (A) (B) (C) (D)   8. (A) (B) (C) (D)

11.

12.

13. (A) (B) (C) (D)   17. (A) (B) (C) (D)   21. (A) (B) (C) (D)
14. (A) (B) (C) (D)   18. (A) (B) (C) (D)   22. (A) (B) (C) (D)
15. (A) (B) (C) (D)   19. (A) (B) (C) (D)
16. (A) (B) (C) (D)   20. (A) (B) (C) (D)

23.

24.

25. Ⓐ Ⓑ Ⓒ Ⓓ   29. Ⓐ Ⓑ Ⓒ Ⓓ   33. Ⓐ Ⓑ Ⓒ Ⓓ
26. Ⓐ Ⓑ Ⓒ Ⓓ   30. Ⓐ Ⓑ Ⓒ Ⓓ   34. Ⓐ Ⓑ Ⓒ Ⓓ
27. Ⓐ Ⓑ Ⓒ Ⓓ   31. Ⓐ Ⓑ Ⓒ Ⓓ
28. Ⓐ Ⓑ Ⓒ Ⓓ   32. Ⓐ Ⓑ Ⓒ Ⓓ

35.

36.

37. (A) (B) (C) (D)   41. (A) (B) (C) (D)   45. (A) (B) (C) (D)
38. (A) (B) (C) (D)   42. (A) (B) (C) (D)   46. (A) (B) (C) (D)
39. (A) (B) (C) (D)   43. (A) (B) (C) (D)
40. (A) (B) (C) (D)   44. (A) (B) (C) (D)

47.

48.

HSPA – Practice Test 2
Answer Sheet

Mathematics

1. Ⓐ Ⓑ Ⓒ Ⓓ   5. Ⓐ Ⓑ Ⓒ Ⓓ   9. Ⓐ Ⓑ Ⓒ Ⓓ
2. Ⓐ Ⓑ Ⓒ Ⓓ   6. Ⓐ Ⓑ Ⓒ Ⓓ   10. Ⓐ Ⓑ Ⓒ Ⓓ
3. Ⓐ Ⓑ Ⓒ Ⓓ   7. Ⓐ Ⓑ Ⓒ Ⓓ
4. Ⓐ Ⓑ Ⓒ Ⓓ   8. Ⓐ Ⓑ Ⓒ Ⓓ

11.

12.

13. Ⓐ Ⓑ Ⓒ Ⓓ   17. Ⓐ Ⓑ Ⓒ Ⓓ   21. Ⓐ Ⓑ Ⓒ Ⓓ
14. Ⓐ Ⓑ Ⓒ Ⓓ   18. Ⓐ Ⓑ Ⓒ Ⓓ   22. Ⓐ Ⓑ Ⓒ Ⓓ
15. Ⓐ Ⓑ Ⓒ Ⓓ   19. Ⓐ Ⓑ Ⓒ Ⓓ
16. Ⓐ Ⓑ Ⓒ Ⓓ   20. Ⓐ Ⓑ Ⓒ Ⓓ

23.

24.

25. Ⓐ Ⓑ Ⓒ Ⓓ   29. Ⓐ Ⓑ Ⓒ Ⓓ   33. Ⓐ Ⓑ Ⓒ Ⓓ
26. Ⓐ Ⓑ Ⓒ Ⓓ   30. Ⓐ Ⓑ Ⓒ Ⓓ   34. Ⓐ Ⓑ Ⓒ Ⓓ
27. Ⓐ Ⓑ Ⓒ Ⓓ   31. Ⓐ Ⓑ Ⓒ Ⓓ
28. Ⓐ Ⓑ Ⓒ Ⓓ   32. Ⓐ Ⓑ Ⓒ Ⓓ

35.

36.

37. Ⓐ Ⓑ Ⓒ Ⓓ   41. Ⓐ Ⓑ Ⓒ Ⓓ   45. Ⓐ Ⓑ Ⓒ Ⓓ
38. Ⓐ Ⓑ Ⓒ Ⓓ   42. Ⓐ Ⓑ Ⓒ Ⓓ   46. Ⓐ Ⓑ Ⓒ Ⓓ
39. Ⓐ Ⓑ Ⓒ Ⓓ   43. Ⓐ Ⓑ Ⓒ Ⓓ
40. Ⓐ Ⓑ Ⓒ Ⓓ   44. Ⓐ Ⓑ Ⓒ Ⓓ

47.

48.

NEW JERSEY

HSPA

High School Proficiency Assessment in
Mathematics

CLASS & HOMEWORK ASSIGNMENTS

Note: Answers and explanations to these Class & Homework Assignments are given in the Teacher's Guide, which is available from REA.

CLASS AND HOMEWORK ASSIGNMENTS

Mathematics

These assignments are provided with five answer choices each, as opposed to the HSPA's four answer choices. This results in a greater challenge and more rigorous preparation.

Integers and Real Numbers, Absolute Value, Order of Operations

Addition

1. Simplify $4 + (-7) + 2 + (-5)$.

   (A) -6 (B) -4 (C) 0 (D) 6 (E) 18

2. Simplify $144 + (-317) + 213$.

   (A) -357 (B) -40 (C) 40 (D) 357 (E) 674

3. Simplify $|4 + (-3)| + |-2|$.

   (A) -2 (B) -1 (C) 1 (D) 3 (E) 9

4. What integer makes the equation $-13 + 12 + 7 + ? = 10$ a true statement?

   (A) -22 (B) -10 (C) 4 (D) 6 (E) 10

5. Simplify $4 + 17 + (-29) + 13 + (-22) + (-3)$.

   (A) -44 (B) -20 (C) 23 (D) 34 (E) 78

Subtraction

6. Simplify $319 - 428$.

   (A) -111 (B) -109 (C) -99 (D) 109 (E) 747

7. Simplify 91,203 – 37,904 + 1,073.

    (A) 54,372   (B) 64,701   (C) 128,034

    (D) 129,107   (E) 130,180

8. Simplify | 43 – 62 | – | – 17 – 3 |.

    (A) – 39   (B) – 19   (C) – 1   (D) 1   (E) 39

9. Simplify – (– 4 – 7) + (– 2).

    (A) – 22   (B) – 13   (C) – 9   (D) 7   (E) 9

10. In Great Smoky Mountains National Park, Mt. LeConte rises from 1,292 feet above sea level to 6,593 feet above sea level. How tall is Mt. LeConte?

    (A) 4,009 ft   (B) 5,301 ft   (C) 5,699 ft

    (D) 6,464 ft   (E) 7,885 ft

Multiplication

11. Simplify – 3 (– 18) (– 1).

    (A) – 108   (B) – 54   (C) – 48   (D) 48   (E) 54

12. Simplify | – 42 | * | 7 |.

    (A) – 294   (B) – 49   (C) – 35   (D) 284   (E) 294

13. Simplify – 6 * 5 (– 10) (– 4) 0 * 2.

    (A) – 2,400   (B) – 240   (C) 0

    (D) 280   (E) 2,700

14. Simplify – | – 6 * 8 |.

    (A) – 48   (B) – 42   (C) 2   (D) 42   (E) 48

15. A city in Georgia had a record low temperature of –3°F one winter. During the same year, a city in Michigan experienced a record low that was nine times the record low set in Georgia. What was the record low in Michigan that year?

    (A) – 31°F   (B) – 27°F   (C) – 21°F

    (D) – 12°F   (E) – 6°F

Division

16. Simplify $-24 \div 8$.

    (A) -4 (B) -3 (C) -2 (D) 3 (E) 4

17. Simplify $(-180) \div (-12)$.

    (A) -30 (B) -15 (C) 1.5 (D) 15 (E) 216

18. Simplify $|-76| \div |-4|$.

    (A) -21 (B) -19 (C) 13 (D) 19 (E) 21.5

19. Simplify $|216 \div (-6)|$.

    (A) -36 (B) -12 (C) 36 (D) 38 (E) 43

20. At the end of the year, a small firm has \$2,996 in its account for bonuses. If the entire amount is equally divided among the 14 employees, how much does each one receive?

    (A) \$107   (B) \$114   (C) \$170   (D) \$210   (E) \$214

Order of Operations

21. Simplify $\dfrac{4+8*2}{5-1}$.

    (A) 4 (B) 5 (C) 6 (D) 8 (E) 12

22. $96 \div 3 \div 4 \div 2 =$

    (A) 65 (B) 64 (C) 16 (D) 8 (E) 4

23. $3 + 4 * 2 - 6 \div 3 =$

    (A) -1 (B) $5/3$ (C) $8/3$ (D) 9 (E) 12

24. $[(4+8)*3] \div 9 =$

    (A) 4 (B) 8 (C) 12 (D) 24 (E) 36

25. $18 + 3 * 4 \div 3 =$

    (A) 3 (B) 5 (C) 10 (D) 22 (E) 28

26. $(29 - 17 + 4) \div 4 + |-2| =$

   (A) $2^2/_3$ (B) 4   (C) $4^2/_3$ (D) 6   (E) 15

27. $(-3) * 5 - 20 \div 4 =$

   (A) -75 (B) -20 (C) -10 (D) $-8^3/_4$ (E) 20

28. $\dfrac{11 * 2 + 2}{16 - 2 * 2} =$

   (A) 11/16   (B) 1   (C) 2   (D) 3 2/3   (E) 4

29. $|-8 - 4| \div 3 * 6 + (-4) =$

   (A) 20   (B) 26   (C) 32   (D) 62   (E) 212

30. $32 \div 2 + 4 - 15 \div 3 =$

   (A) 0   (B) 7   (C) 15   (D) 23   (E) 63

Exponents, Power to a Power

1. $2^2 \cdot 2^5 \cdot 2^3 =$

   (A) 2^{10} (B) 4^{10} (C) 8^{10} (D) 2^{30} (E) 8^{30}

2. $6^6 \cdot 6^2 \cdot 6^4 =$

   (A) 18^8 (B) 18^{12} (C) 6^{12} (D) 6^{48} (E) 18^{48}

Division

Simplify:

3. $6^5 \div 6^3 =$

   (A) 0   (B) 1   (C) 6   (D) 12   (E) 6^2

4. $c^{17}d^{12}e^4 \div c^{12}d^8e =$

   (A) $c^4d^5e^3$ (B) $c^4d^4e^3$ (C) $c^5d^8e^4$

   (D) $c^5d^4e^3$ (E) $c^5d^4e^4$

5. $(4^3)^5 =$

   (A) 4^2 (B) 2^{15} (C) 4^8 (D) 20^3 (E) 4^{15}

6. $(a^4b^3)^2 =$

   (A) $(ab)^9$ (B) a^8b^6 (C) $(ab)^{24}$

   (D) a^6b^5 (E) $2a^4b^3$

Ratios and Proportions

1. Solve for n : $\dfrac{4}{n} = \dfrac{8}{5}$

   (A) 10   (B) 8   (C) 6   (D) 2.5   (E) 2

2. Solve for n: $n : 12 = 3 : 4$.

   (A) 8   (B) 1   (C) 9   (D) 4   (E) 10

3. Four out of every five students at West High take a mathematics course. If the enrollment at West is 785, how many students take mathematics?

   (A) 628   (B) 157   (C) 705   (D) 655   (E) 247

4. At a factory, three out of every 1,000 parts produced are defective. In a day, the factory can produce 25,000 parts. How many of these parts would be defective?

   (A) 7   (B) 75   (C) 750   (D) 7,500   (E) 75,000

5. A summer league softball team won 28 out of the 32 games they played. What is the ratio of games won to games played?

   (A) $4 : 5$ (B) $3 : 4$ (C) $7 : 8$ (D) $2 : 3$ (E) $1 : 8$

6. A family has a monthly income of $1,250, but they spend $450 a month on rent. What is the ratio of the amount of income to the amount paid for rent?

   (A) $16 : 25$ (B) $25 : 9$ (C) $25 : 16$ (D) $9 : 25$ (E) $36 : 100$

7.	A student attends classes 7.5 hours a day and works a part-time job for 3.5 hours a day. She knows she must get 7 hours of sleep a night. Write the ratio of the number of free hours in this student's day to the total number of hours in a day.

   (A) 1 : 3   (B) 4 : 3   (C) 8 : 24   (D) 1 : 4   (E) 5 : 12

Intersecting Lines and Angles

1.	Determine *x*.

(A) 21°   (B) 23°   (C) 51°

(D) 102°   (E) 153°

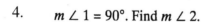

2.	Find *x*.

(A) 8   (B) 11.75   (C) 21

(D) 23   (E) 32

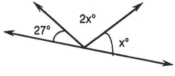

3.	Find *z*.

(A) 29°   (B) 54°   (C) 61°

(D) 88°   (E) 92°

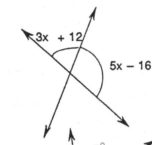

Perpendicular Lines

4.	*m* ∠ 1 = 90°. Find *m* ∠ 2.

(A) 80°   (B) 90°   (C) 100°

(D) 135°   (E) 180°

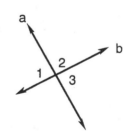

5. $\overline{CD} \perp \overline{EF}$. If $m \angle 1 = 2x$, $m \angle 2 = 30°$, and $m \angle 3 = x$, find x.

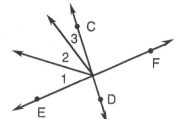

(A) 5°   (B) 10°   (C) 12°

(D) 20°   (E) 25°

6. In the figure, $p \perp t$ and $q \perp t$. Which of the following statements is false?

(A) $\angle 1 \cong \angle 4$

(B) $\angle 2 \cong \angle 3$

(C) $m\angle 2 + m \angle 3 = m \angle 4 + m \angle 6$

(D) $m \angle 5 + m \angle 6 = 180°$

(E) $m \angle 2 > m \angle 5$

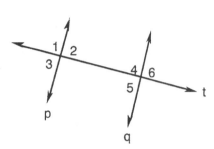

Parallel Lines

7. In the figure, $p \, || \, q \, || \, r$. Find $m \angle 7$.

(A) 27°   (B) 33°   (C) 47°

(D) 57°   (E) 64°

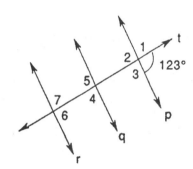

8. If $m \, || \, n$, which of the following statements is false?

(A) $\angle 2 \cong \angle 5$

(B) $\angle 3 \cong \angle 6$

(C) $m\angle 4 + m \angle 5 = 180 °$

(D) $\angle 2 \cong \angle 8$

(E) $m \angle 7 + m \angle 3 = 180°$

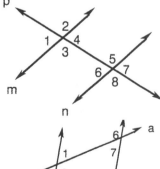

9. If $a \, || \, b$ and $c \, || \, d$, find $m \angle 5$.

(A) 55°   (B) 65°   (C) 75°

(D) 95°   (E) 125°

Triangles

Angle Measures

1.   In △ *PQR*, ∠ *Q* is a right angle. Find *m* ∠*R*.

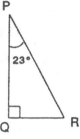

(A)   27°   (B)   33°   (C)   54°

(D)   67°   (E)   157°

2.   △ *MNO* is isosceles. If the vertex angle, ∠ *N*, has a measure of 96°, find the measure of ∠ *M*.

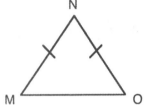

(A)   21°   (B)   42°   (C)   64°

(D)   84°   (E)   96°

3.   Find *x*.

(A)   15°   (B)   25°   (C)   30°

(D)   45°   (E)   90°

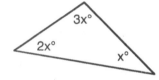

4.   Find *m* ∠1.

(A)   40   (B)   66   (C)   74

(D)   114   (E)   140

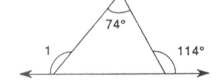

5.   △ *ABC* is a right triangle with a right angle at *B*. △ *BDC* is a right triangle with right angle ∠ *BDC*. If *m* ∠*C* = 36, find *m* ∠*A*.

(A)   18   (B)   36   (C)   54

(D)   72   (E)   180

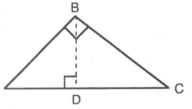

Similar Triangles

6.   The two triangles shown are similar. Find *b*.

(A)   2 2/3   (B)   3   (C)   4

(D)   16   (E)   24

7. The two triangles shown are similar. Find $m \angle 1$.

(A) 48   (B) 53   (C) 74

(D) 127   (E) 180

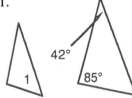

8. The two triangles shown are similar. Find a and b.

(A) 5 and 10   (B) 4 and 8

(C) 4 2/3 and 7 1/3   (D) 5 and 8

(E) 5 1/3 and 8

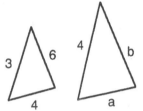

9. The perimeter of $\triangle LXR$ is 45 and the perimeter of $\triangle ABC$ is 27. If $LX = 15$, find the length of AB.

(A) 9   (B) 15   (C) 27

(D) 45   (E) 72

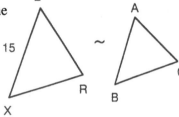

10. Find b.

(A) 9   (B) 15   (C) 20

(D) 45   (E) 60

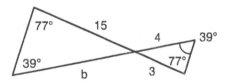

Area

11. Find the area of $\triangle MNO$.

(A) 22   (B) 49   (C) 56

(D) 84   (E) 112

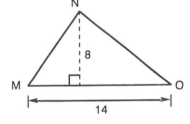

12. Find the area of $\triangle PQR$.

(A) 31.5   (B) 38.5   (C) 53

(D) 77   (E) 82.5

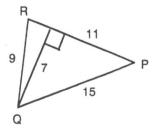

13. Find the area of Δ *STU*.

(A) $4\sqrt{2}$ (B) $8\sqrt{2}$ (C) $12\sqrt{2}$

(D) $16\sqrt{2}$ (E) $32\sqrt{2}$

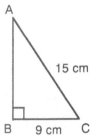

14. Find the area of Δ *ABC*.

(A) 54 cm² (B) 81 cm² (C) 108 cm²

(D) 135 cm² (E) 180 cm²

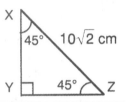

15. Find the area of Δ *XYZ*.

(A) 20 cm² (B) 50 cm² (C) $50\sqrt{2}$ cm²

(D) 100 cm² (E) 200 cm²

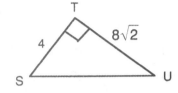

Quadrilaterals

Parallelograms, Rectangles, Rhombi, Squares, Trapezoids

1. In parallelogram *WXYZ*, *WX* = 14, *WZ* = 6, *ZY* = 3*x* + 5, and *XY* = 2*y* − 4. Find *x* and *y*.

(A) 3 and 5 (B) 4 and 5 (C) 4 and 6

(D) 6 and 10 (E) 6 and 14

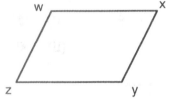

2. Quadrilateral *ABCD* is a parellelogram. If *m* ∠ *B* = 6*x* + 2 and *m* ∠ *D* = 98, find *x*.

(A) 12 (B) 16 (C) 16 2/3

(D) 18 (E) 20

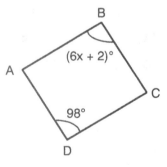

3. Find the area of parallelogram *MNOP*.

(A) 19   (B) 32   (C) $32\sqrt{3}$

(D) 44   (E) $44\sqrt{3}$

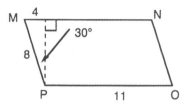

4. Find the area of rectangle *UVXY*.

(A) 17 cm²   (B) 34 cm²   (C) 35 cm²

(D) 70 cm²   (E) 140 cm²

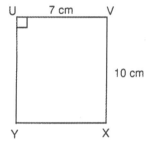

5. Find *x* in rectangle *BCDE* if the diagonal *EC* is 17 mm.

(A) 6.55 mm (B) 8 mm   (C) 8.5 mm

(D) 17 mm   (E) 34 mm

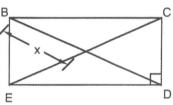

6. In rhombus *DEFG*, *DE* = 7 cm. Find the perimeter of the rhombus.

(A) 14 cm   (B) 28 cm   (C) 42 cm

(D) 49 cm   (E) 56 cm

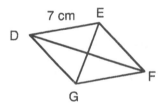

7. In rhombus *RHOM*, the diagonal $\overline{RO}$ is 8 cm and the diagonal $\overline{HM}$ is 12 cm. Find the area of the rhombus.

(A) 20 cm²   (B) 40 cm²   (C) 48 cm²

(D) 68 cm²   (E) 96 cm²

8. In rhombus *GHIJ*, *GI* = 6 cm and *HJ* = 8 cm. Find the length of *GH*.

(A) 3 cm   (B) 4 cm   (C) 5 cm

(D) $4\sqrt{3}$ cm   (E) 14 cm

9. In rhombus *CDEF*, *CD* is 13 mm and *DX* is 5 mm. Find the area of the rhombus.

    (A) 31 mm² (B) 60 mm² (C) 78 mm²

    (D) 120 mm² (E) 260 mm²

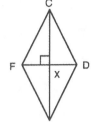

10. Quadrilateral *ATUV* is a square. If the perimeter of the square is 44 cm, find the length of $\overline{AT}$.

    (A) 4 cm (B) 11 cm (C) 22 cm (D) 30 cm (E) 40 cm

11. The area of square *XYZW* is 196 cm². Find the perimeter of the square.

    (A) 28 cm (B) 42 cm (C) 56 cm

    (D) 98 cm (E) 196 cm.

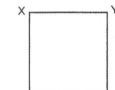

12. In square *MNOP*, *MN* is 6 cm. Find the length of diagonal $\overline{MO}$.

    (A) 6 cm (B) $6\sqrt{2}$ cm (C) $6\sqrt{3}$ cm

    (D) $6\sqrt{6}$ cm (E) 12 cm

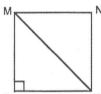

13. In square *ABCD*, *AB* = 3 cm. Find the area of the square.

    (A) 9 cm² (B) 12 cm² (C) 15 cm²

    (D) 18 cm² (E) 21 cm²

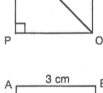

14. *ABCD* is an isosceles trapezoid. Find the perimeter.

    (A) 21 cm (B) 27 cm (C) 30 cm

    (D) 50 cm (E) 54 cm

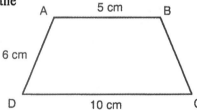

15. Find the area of trapezoid *MNOP*.

(A) $(17 + 3\sqrt{3})$ mm²

(B) 33/2 mm²

(C) $33\sqrt{3}/2$ mm²

(D) 33 mm²

(E) $33\sqrt{3}$ mm²

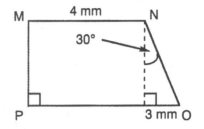

16. Trapezoid *XYZW* is isosceles. If $m \angle W = 58$ and $m \angle Z = 4x - 6$, find *x*.

(A) 8   (B) 12   (C) 13

(D) 16   (E) 58

Circles

1. The circumference of circle *H* is 20π cm. Find the length of the radius.

(A) 10 cm   (B) 20 cm   (C) 10π cm   (D) 15π cm   (E) 20π cm

2. The circumference of circle *A* is how many millimeters larger than the circumference of circle *B*?

(A) 3   (B) 6   (C) 3π

(D) 6π (E) 7π

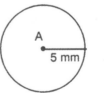

3. If the diameter of circle *X* is 9 cm and if $\pi = 3.14$, find the circumference of the circle to the nearest tenth.

(A) 9 cm   (B) 14.1 cm   (C) 21.1 cm   (D) 24.6 cm   (E) 28.3 cm

4. Find the area of circle *I*.

(A) 22 mm²   (B) 121 mm²

(C) 121π mm²   (D) 132 mm²

(E) 132π mm²

5. The diameter of circle Z is 27 mm. Find the area of the circle.

(A) 91.125 mm^2 (B) 182.25 mm^2 (C) 191.5π mm^2

(D) 182.25π mm^2 (E) 729 mm^2

6. The area of circle X is 144π mm^2 while the area of circle Y is 81π mm^2. Write the ratio of the radius of circle X to that of circle Y.

(A) 3 : 4   (B) 4 : 3   (C) 9 : 12   (D) 27 : 12   (E) 18 : 24

7. The circumference of circle M is 18π cm. Find the area of the circle.

(A) 18π cm^2 (B) 81 cm^2 (C) 36 cm^2 (D) 36π cm^2 (E) 81π cm^2

8. In two concentric circles, the smaller circle has a radius of 3 mm while the larger circle has a radius of 5 mm. Find the area of the shaded region.

(A) 2π mm^2 (B) 8π mm^2 (C) 13π mm^2

(D) 16π mm^2 (E) 26π mm^2

9. The radius of the smaller of two concentric circles is 5 cm while the radius of the larger circle is 7 cm. Determine the area of the shaded region.

(A) 7π cm^2 (B) 24π cm^2 (C) 25π cm^2

(D) 36π cm^2 (E) 49π cm^2

10. Find the measure of arc MN if $m \angle MON$ = 62°.

(A) 16°   (B) 32°   (C) 59°

(D) 62°   (E) 124°

11. Find the measure of arc AXC.

(A) 150°   (B) 160°   (C) 180°

(D) 270°   (E) 360°

12. If arc *MXP* = 236°, find the measure of arc *MP*.

(A) 62°   (B) 124°   (C) 236°

(D) 270°   (E) 360°

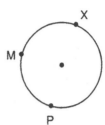

13. In circle *S*, major arc *PQR* has a measure of 298°. Find the measure of the central angle ∠ *PSR*.

(A) 62°   (B) 124°   (C) 149°

(D) 298°   (E) 360°

14. Find the measure of arc *XY* in circle *W*.

(A) 40°   (B) 120°   (C) 140°

(D) 180°   (E) 220°

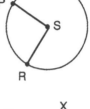

15. Find the area of the sector shown.

(A) 4 cm²   (B) 2π cm²   (C) 16 cm²

(D) 8π cm²   (E) 16π cm²

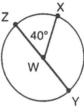

16. Find the area of the shaded region.

(A) 10   (B) 5π   (C) 25

(D) 20π   (E) 25π

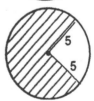

17. If the area of the square is 100 cm², find the area of the sector.

(A) 10π cm²   (B) 25 cm²   (C) 25π cm²

(D) 100 cm²   (E) 100π cm²

Solids

1. Find the surface area of the rectangular prism shown.

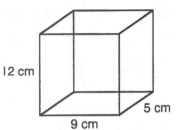

(A) 138 cm² (B) 336 cm² (C) 381 cm²

(D) 426 cm² (E) 540 cm²

2. Find the volume of the rectangular storage tank shown.

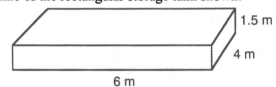

(A) 24 m³ (B) 36 m³ (C) 38 m³ (D) 42 m³ (E) 45 m³

3. The lateral area of a cube is 100 cm². Find the length of an edge of the cube.

(A) 4 cm (B) 5 cm (C) 10 cm (D) 12 cm (E) 15 cm

Coordinate Geometry

1. Which point shown has the coordinates (– 3, 2)?

(A) A (B) B (C) C

(D) D (E) E

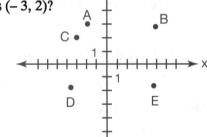

2. Name the coordinates of point A.

(A) (4, 3) (B) (3, – 4) (C) (3, 4)

(D) (– 4, 3) (E) (4, – 3)

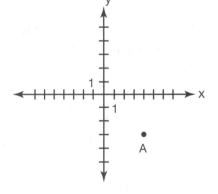

3.   Which point shown has the coordinates (2.5, –1)?

(A) M   (B) N   (C) P

(D) Q   (E) R

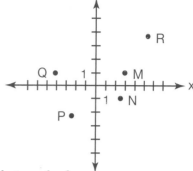

4.   The correct *x*-coordinate for point *H* is what number?

(A) 3   (B) 4   (C) – 3

(D) – 4   (E) – 5

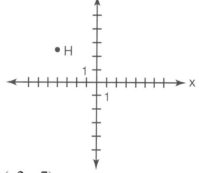

5.   Find the distance between (4, –7) and (–2, –7).

(A) 4   (B) 6   (C) 7   (D) 14   (E) 15

6.   Find the distance between (3, 8) and (5, 11).

(A) 2   (B) 3   (C) $\sqrt{13}$ (D) $\sqrt{15}$ (E) $3\sqrt{3}$

7.   Find the distance between the point (–4, 2) and (3, –5).

(A) 3   (B) $3\sqrt{3}$ (C) 7   (D) $7\sqrt{2}$ (E) $7\sqrt{3}$

8.   The distance between points *A* and *B* is 10 units. If *A* has coordinates (4, –6) and *B* has coordinates (–2, *y*), determine the value of *y*.

(A) –6   (B) –2   (C) 0   (D) 1   (E) 2

9.   Find the midpoint between the points (–2, 6) and (4, 8).

(A) (3, 7)   (B) (1, 7)   (C) (3, 1)   (D) (1, 1)   (E) (–3, 7)

10. Find the coordinates of the midpoint btween the points (–5, 7) and (3, –1)

(A) (–4, 4)   (B) (3, –1)   (C) (1, –3)   (D) (–1, 3)   (E) (4, –4)

Probability

1. A deck of playing cards is thoroughly shuffled and a card is drawn from the deck. What is the probability that the card drawn is the ace of diamonds?

    (A) 1/26   (B) 2/3   (C) 1/52   (D) 1/26   (E) 1/64

2. A box contains 7 red, 5 white, and 4 black balls. What is the probablility of drawing at random one black ball?

    (A) 4/5   (B) 7/4   (C) 1/4   (D) 1/8   (E) 1/2

3. In a single throw of a single die, find the probability of throwing either a 2 or a 5.

    (A) 2/5   (B) 7/4   (C) 1/3   (D) 1/6   (E) 1/5

4. A bag contains 4 white balls, 6 black balls, 3 red balls, and 8 green balls. If one ball is drawn from the bag, find the probability that it will either be white or green.

    (A) 4/7   (B) 2/3   (C) 3/4   (D) 1/3   (E) 4/3

5. A penny is to be tossed 3 times. What is the probability that there will be 2 heads and 1 tail?

    (A) 2/3   (B) 3/2   (C) 1/3   (D) 3/8   (E) 8/3

6. What is the chance of throwing a number greater than 4 with an ordinary die whose faces are numbered from 1 to 6?

    (A) 1/3   (B) 2/3   (C) 1/10   (D) 1/4   (E) 1/6

7. A bag contains 10 red, 15 green, and 5 yellow beads. If a single bead is drawn from the bag, what is the probability that the bead is not red?

    (A) 2/1   (B) 1/3   (C) 1/2   (D) 1/30   (E) 2/3

8. A traffic count at a highway junction revealed that out of 5,000 cars that passed through the junction in one week, 3,000 turned to the right. Find the probability that a car will turn to the left.

    (A) 3/5   (B) 3/8   (C) 5/3

    (D) 2/5   (E) 8/3

Inequalities

DIRECTIONS: Find the solution set for each inequality.

1. $3m + 2 < 7$

    (A) $m \geq {}^5/_3$ (B) $m \leq 2$ (C) $m < 2$

    (D) $m > 2$ (E) $m < {}^5/_3$

2. ${}^1/_2 x - 3 \leq 1$

    (A) $-4 \leq x \leq 8$ (B) $x \geq -8$ (C) $x \leq 8$

    (D) $2 \leq x \leq 8$ (E) $x \geq 8$

3. $-3p + 1 \geq 16$

    (A) $p \geq -5$ (B) $p \geq \dfrac{-17}{3}$ (C) $p \leq \dfrac{-17}{3}$

    (D) $p \leq -5$ (E) $p \geq 5$

4. $-6 < {}^2/_3 r + 6 \leq 2$

    (A) $-6 < r \leq -3$ (B) $-18 < r \leq -6$ (C) $r \geq -6$

    (D) $-2 < r \leq {}^{-4}/_3$ (E) $r \leq -6$

5. $0 < 2 - y < 6$

    (A) $-4 < y < 2$ (B) $-4 < y < 0$ (C) $-4 < y < -2$

    (D) $-2 < y < 4$ (E) $0 < y < 4$

ARITHMETIC DIAGNOSTIC TEST

1. Ⓐ Ⓑ Ⓒ Ⓓ Ⓔ
2. Ⓐ Ⓑ Ⓒ Ⓓ Ⓔ
3. Ⓐ Ⓑ Ⓒ Ⓓ Ⓔ
4. Ⓐ Ⓑ Ⓒ Ⓓ Ⓔ
5. Ⓐ Ⓑ Ⓒ Ⓓ Ⓔ
6. Ⓐ Ⓑ Ⓒ Ⓓ Ⓔ
7. Ⓐ Ⓑ Ⓒ Ⓓ Ⓔ
8. Ⓐ Ⓑ Ⓒ Ⓓ Ⓔ
9. Ⓐ Ⓑ Ⓒ Ⓓ Ⓔ
10. Ⓐ Ⓑ Ⓒ Ⓓ Ⓔ
11. Ⓐ Ⓑ Ⓒ Ⓓ Ⓔ
12. Ⓐ Ⓑ Ⓒ Ⓓ Ⓔ
13. Ⓐ Ⓑ Ⓒ Ⓓ Ⓔ
14. Ⓐ Ⓑ Ⓒ Ⓓ Ⓔ
15. Ⓐ Ⓑ Ⓒ Ⓓ Ⓔ
16. Ⓐ Ⓑ Ⓒ Ⓓ Ⓔ
17. Ⓐ Ⓑ Ⓒ Ⓓ Ⓔ
18. Ⓐ Ⓑ Ⓒ Ⓓ Ⓔ
19. Ⓐ Ⓑ Ⓒ Ⓓ Ⓔ
20. Ⓐ Ⓑ Ⓒ Ⓓ Ⓔ
21. Ⓐ Ⓑ Ⓒ Ⓓ Ⓔ
22. Ⓐ Ⓑ Ⓒ Ⓓ Ⓔ
23. Ⓐ Ⓑ Ⓒ Ⓓ Ⓔ
24. Ⓐ Ⓑ Ⓒ Ⓓ Ⓔ
25. Ⓐ Ⓑ Ⓒ Ⓓ Ⓔ

26. Ⓐ Ⓑ Ⓒ Ⓓ Ⓔ
27. Ⓐ Ⓑ Ⓒ Ⓓ Ⓔ
28. Ⓐ Ⓑ Ⓒ Ⓓ Ⓔ
29. Ⓐ Ⓑ Ⓒ Ⓓ Ⓔ
30. Ⓐ Ⓑ Ⓒ Ⓓ Ⓔ
31. Ⓐ Ⓑ Ⓒ Ⓓ Ⓔ
32. Ⓐ Ⓑ Ⓒ Ⓓ Ⓔ
33. Ⓐ Ⓑ Ⓒ Ⓓ Ⓔ
34. Ⓐ Ⓑ Ⓒ Ⓓ Ⓔ
35. Ⓐ Ⓑ Ⓒ Ⓓ Ⓔ
36. Ⓐ Ⓑ Ⓒ Ⓓ Ⓔ
37. Ⓐ Ⓑ Ⓒ Ⓓ Ⓔ
38. Ⓐ Ⓑ Ⓒ Ⓓ Ⓔ
39. Ⓐ Ⓑ Ⓒ Ⓓ Ⓔ
40. Ⓐ Ⓑ Ⓒ Ⓓ Ⓔ
41. Ⓐ Ⓑ Ⓒ Ⓓ Ⓔ
42. Ⓐ Ⓑ Ⓒ Ⓓ Ⓔ
43. Ⓐ Ⓑ Ⓒ Ⓓ Ⓔ
44. Ⓐ Ⓑ Ⓒ Ⓓ Ⓔ
45. Ⓐ Ⓑ Ⓒ Ⓓ Ⓔ
46. Ⓐ Ⓑ Ⓒ Ⓓ Ⓔ
47. Ⓐ Ⓑ Ⓒ Ⓓ Ⓔ
48. Ⓐ Ⓑ Ⓒ Ⓓ Ⓔ
49. Ⓐ Ⓑ Ⓒ Ⓓ Ⓔ
50. Ⓐ Ⓑ Ⓒ Ⓓ Ⓔ

Arithmetic Diagnostic Test

This diagnostic test is designed to help you determine your strengths and your weaknesses in arithmetic. Follow the directions for each part and check your work.

1. What part of three fourths is one tenth?

    (A) $^1/_8$ (B) $^{15}/_2$ (C) $^2/_{15}$

    (D) $^3/_{40}$ (E) None of the above

2. One number is 2 more than 3 times another. Their sum is 22. Find the numbers.

    (A) 8, 14   (B) 2, 20   (C) 5, 17

    (D) 4, 18   (E) 10, 12

3. What is the median of the following group of scores?

    27, 27, 26, 26, 26, 26, 18, 13, 36, 36, 30, 30, 30, 27, 29

    (A) 30   (B) 26   (C) 25.4

    (D) 27   (E) 36

4. What percent of 260 is 13?

    (A) .05%   (B) 5%   (C) 50%

    (D) .5%   (E) 20%

5. Subtract: $4\,^1/_3 - 1\,^5/_6$

    (A) $3\,^2/_3$ (B) $2^1/_2$ (C) $3^1/_2$

    (D) $2\,^1/_6$ (E) None of the above

6. What is the product of $(\sqrt{3} + 6)$ and $(\sqrt{3} - 2)$?

    (A) $9 + 4\sqrt{3}$ (B) -9 (C) $-9 + 4\sqrt{3}$

    (D) $-9 + 2\sqrt{3}$ (E) 9

7. The number missing in the series, 2, 6, 12, 20, x, 42, 56 is:

   (A) 36   (B) 24   (C) 30

   (D) 38   (E) 40

8. What is the value of the following expression: $\cfrac{1}{1+\cfrac{1}{1+\cfrac{1}{4}}}$

   (A) $^9/_5$ (B) $^5/_9$ (C) $^1/_2$

   (D) 2   (E) 4

9. Which of the following has the smallest value?

   (A) $^1/_{0.2}$ (B) $^{0.1}/_2$ (C) $^{0.2}/_1$

   (D) $^{0.2}/_{0.1}$ (E) $^2/_{0.1}$

10. Which is the smallest number?

    (A) $(5 \cdot 10^{-3}) / (3 \cdot 10^{-3})$ (B) $.3 / .2$

    (C) $.3 / (3 \cdot 10^{-3})$ (D) $(5 \cdot 10^{-2}) / .1$

    (E) $.3 / (3 \cdot 10^{-1})$

11. $10^3 + 10^5 =$

    (A) 10^8 (B) 10^{15} (C) 20^8

    (D) 2^{15} (E) 101,000

12. How many digits are in the standard numeral for $2^{31} \cdot 5^{27}$?

    (A) 31   (B) 29   (C) 28

    (D) 26   (E) 25

13. $475,826 \cdot 521,653 + 524,174 \cdot 521,653 =$

    (A) 621,592,047,600   (B) 519,697,450,000

    (C) 495,652,831,520   (D) 521,653,000,000

    (E) 524,174,000,000

14. How many ways can you make change for a quarter?

 (A) 8   (B) 9   (C) 10

 (D) 12   (E) 14

15. The sixtieth digit in the decimal representation of $1/7$ is

 (A) 1   (B) 4   (C) 2

 (D) 5   (E) 7

16. What is the least prime number which is a divisor of $7^9 + 11^{25}$?

 (A) 1   (B) 2   (C) 3

 (D) 5   (E) $7^9 + 11^{25}$

17. Evaluate $10 - 5[2^3 + 27 \div 3 - 2(8 - 10)]$

 (A) -95 (B) 105   (C) 65

 (D) -55 (E) -85

18. Fifteen percent of what number is 60?

 (A) 9   (B) 51   (C) 69

 (D) 200   (E) 400

19. Which is the largest fraction: $1/5$, $2/9$, $2/11$, $4/19$, $4/17$?

 (A) $1/5$ (B) $2/9$ (C) $2/11$

 (D) $4/19$ (E) $4/17$

20. How many of the scores 10, 20, 30, 35, 55 are larger than their arithmetic mean score?

 (A) None   (B) One   (C) Two

 (D) Three   (E) Four

21. Evaluate $(2^{1-\sqrt{3}})^{1+\sqrt{3}}$

 (A) 4   (B) -4 (C) 16

 (D) $1/2$ (E) $1/4$

22. $\dfrac{2^{100} + 2^{98}}{2^{100} - 2^{98}} = .$

    (A) 2^{198} (B) 2^{99} (C) 64

    (D) 4 (E) $5/3$

23. What is the least natural number that is a multiple of each number from 1 to 10?

    (A) 3,628,800 (B) 5,040 (C) 840

    (D) 1,260 (E) 2,520

24. If in $\triangle ABC$, $AB = BC$ and angle A has measure 46°, then angle B has measure

    (A) 46° (B) 92° (C) 88°

    (D) 56° (E) 23°

25. What is the last digit in the number 3^{2000}?

    (A) 0 (B) 1 (C) 3

    (D) 7 (E) 9

26. In the set of integers 1000, 1001, 1002, ..., 9998, 9999, how many of the numbers do not contain the digit 5?

    (A) 6,561 (B) 5,000 (C) 9,000

    (D) 4,500 (E) 5,832

27. $15,561 \div 25 + 9,439 \div 25 =$

    (A) 997 (B) 1,000 (C) 1,002

    (D) 1,005 (E) 1,005.08

28. What is the units digit for 4^{891}?

    (A) 4 (B) 6 (C) 8

    (D) 0 (E) 1

29. $\dfrac{1}{1\cdot2}+\dfrac{1}{2\cdot3}+\dfrac{1}{3\cdot4}+\ldots+\dfrac{1}{99\cdot100}=$.

   (A) $^{49}/_{50}$ (B) $^{74}/_{75}$ (C) $^{98}/_{99}$

   (D) $^{99}/_{100}$ (E) $^{101}/_{100}$

30. $1+2+3+4+\ldots+99=$

   (A) 4,700   (B) 4,750   (C) 4,850

   (D) 4,900   (E) 4,950

31. The decimal $.24\overline{24}$ expressed as a fraction is

   (A) $^{8}/_{33}$ (B) $^{6}/_{25}$ (C) $^{1}/_{4}$

   (D) $^{303}/_{1250}$ (E) $^{121}/_{500}$

32. $\dfrac{2^{-4}+2^{-1}}{2^{-3}}=$

   (A) $9/2^{7}$ (B) $9/2^{-1}$ (C) $1/2$

   (D) 2^{-3} (E) $9/2$

33. What is the smallest positive number that leaves a remainder of 2 when the number is divided by 3, 4, or 5?

   (A) 22   (B) 42   (C) 62

   (D) 122   (E) 182

34. What part of three eighths is one tenth?

   (A) $^{1}/_{8}$ (B) $^{15}/_{2}$ (C) $^{4}/_{15}$

   (D) $^{3}/_{40}$ (E) None of the above

35. $(^{2}/_{3})+(^{5}/_{9})=$

   (A) $^{7}/_{12}$ (B) $^{11}/_{9}$ (C) $^{7}/_{3}$

   (D) $^{7}/_{9}$ (E) $^{11}/_{3}$

36. Add $^3/_6 + ^2/_6$.

    (A) $^1/_{12}$ (B) $^5/_6$ (C) $^5/_{12}$

    (D) $^8/_9$ (E) $^9/_8$

37. Change 125.937% to a decimal.

    (A) 1.25937   (B)   12.5937   (C)   125.937

    (D) 1259.37   (E)   12593.7

38. What is the ratio of 8 feet to 28 inches?

    (A) $^1/_7$ (B) $^7/_1$ (C) $^{24}/_7$

    (D) $^6/_7$ (E) $^7/_2$

39. Using order of operations, solve: 3 * 6 – 12/2 =

    (A) – 9   (B) 3   (C) 6

    (D) 12   (E) 18

40. The most economical price among the following prices is

    (A) 10 oz. for 16¢   (B) 2 oz. for 3¢

    (C) 4 oz. for 7¢   (D) 20 oz. for 34¢

    (E) 8 oz. for 13¢

41. Change $4^5/_6$ to an improper fraction.

    (A) $^5/_{24}$ (B) $^9/_6$ (C) $^{29}/_6$

    (D) $^{30}/_4$ (E) $^{120}/_6$

42. If the sum of four consecutive integers is 226, then the smallest of these numbers is

    (A) 55   (B) 56   (C) 57   (D) 58   (E) 59

43. How much time is left on the parking meter shown below?

1/2 hr.

   (A) 8 minutes (B)   9 minutes (C) 10 minutes
   (D) 12 minutes (E)   15 minutes

44. $15,561 \div 25 - 9,561 \div 25 =$
   (A) 997   (B) 240   (C) 1,002
   (D) 1,005   (E) 1,005.08

45. $4\% \cdot 4\% =$
   (A) 0.0016%   (B)   0.16%   (C) 1.6%
   (D) 16%   (E)   160%

46. Which of the following numbers is not between $.\overline{85}$ and $.\overline{86}$?
   (A) $\overline{.851}$ (B) $\overline{.859}$ (C) .859
   (D) $\overline{.861}$ (E) .861

47. Change the fraction $^7/_8$ to a decimal.
   (A) .666   (B) .75   (C) .777
   (D) .875   (E) 1.142

48. $\sqrt{75} - 3\sqrt{48} + \sqrt{147} =$
   (A) $3\sqrt{3}$ (B) $7\sqrt{3}$ (C) 0   (D) 3   (E) $\sqrt{3}$

49. The following ratio: 40 seconds : $1^1/_2$ minutes : $^1/_6$ hour, can be expressed in lowest terms as
   (A) $4 : 9 : 60$ (B) $4 : 9 : 6$ (C) $40 : 90 : 60$
   (D) $^2/_3 : 1^1/_2 : 10$ (E) $60 : 9 : 4$

50. Simplify $\left(6\sqrt{7} + 4\sqrt{7}\right)$:
   (A) $10\sqrt{7}$ (B) $15\sqrt{7} - \sqrt{5}$ (C) $15\sqrt{21} - \sqrt{5}$
   (D) $15\sqrt{16}$ (E)   60

ALGEBRA DIAGNOSTIC TEST

1. Ⓐ Ⓑ Ⓒ Ⓓ Ⓔ
2. Ⓐ Ⓑ Ⓒ Ⓓ Ⓔ
3. Ⓐ Ⓑ Ⓒ Ⓓ Ⓔ
4. Ⓐ Ⓑ Ⓒ Ⓓ Ⓔ
5. Ⓐ Ⓑ Ⓒ Ⓓ Ⓔ
6. Ⓐ Ⓑ Ⓒ Ⓓ Ⓔ
7. Ⓐ Ⓑ Ⓒ Ⓓ Ⓔ
8. Ⓐ Ⓑ Ⓒ Ⓓ Ⓔ
9. Ⓐ Ⓑ Ⓒ Ⓓ Ⓔ
10. Ⓐ Ⓑ Ⓒ Ⓓ Ⓔ
11. Ⓐ Ⓑ Ⓒ Ⓓ Ⓔ
12. Ⓐ Ⓑ Ⓒ Ⓓ Ⓔ
13. Ⓐ Ⓑ Ⓒ Ⓓ Ⓔ
14. Ⓐ Ⓑ Ⓒ Ⓓ Ⓔ
15. Ⓐ Ⓑ Ⓒ Ⓓ Ⓔ
16. Ⓐ Ⓑ Ⓒ Ⓓ Ⓔ
17. Ⓐ Ⓑ Ⓒ Ⓓ Ⓔ
18. Ⓐ Ⓑ Ⓒ Ⓓ Ⓔ
19. Ⓐ Ⓑ Ⓒ Ⓓ Ⓔ
20. Ⓐ Ⓑ Ⓒ Ⓓ Ⓔ
21. Ⓐ Ⓑ Ⓒ Ⓓ Ⓔ
22. Ⓐ Ⓑ Ⓒ Ⓓ Ⓔ
23. Ⓐ Ⓑ Ⓒ Ⓓ Ⓔ
24. Ⓐ Ⓑ Ⓒ Ⓓ Ⓔ
25. Ⓐ Ⓑ Ⓒ Ⓓ Ⓔ

26. Ⓐ Ⓑ Ⓒ Ⓓ Ⓔ
27. Ⓐ Ⓑ Ⓒ Ⓓ Ⓔ
28. Ⓐ Ⓑ Ⓒ Ⓓ Ⓔ
29. Ⓐ Ⓑ Ⓒ Ⓓ Ⓔ
30. Ⓐ Ⓑ Ⓒ Ⓓ Ⓔ
31. Ⓐ Ⓑ Ⓒ Ⓓ Ⓔ
32. Ⓐ Ⓑ Ⓒ Ⓓ Ⓔ
33. Ⓐ Ⓑ Ⓒ Ⓓ Ⓔ
34. Ⓐ Ⓑ Ⓒ Ⓓ Ⓔ
35. Ⓐ Ⓑ Ⓒ Ⓓ Ⓔ
36. Ⓐ Ⓑ Ⓒ Ⓓ Ⓔ
37. Ⓐ Ⓑ Ⓒ Ⓓ Ⓔ
38. Ⓐ Ⓑ Ⓒ Ⓓ Ⓔ
39. Ⓐ Ⓑ Ⓒ Ⓓ Ⓔ
40. Ⓐ Ⓑ Ⓒ Ⓓ Ⓔ
41. Ⓐ Ⓑ Ⓒ Ⓓ Ⓔ
42. Ⓐ Ⓑ Ⓒ Ⓓ Ⓔ
43. Ⓐ Ⓑ Ⓒ Ⓓ Ⓔ
44. Ⓐ Ⓑ Ⓒ Ⓓ Ⓔ
45. Ⓐ Ⓑ Ⓒ Ⓓ Ⓔ
46. Ⓐ Ⓑ Ⓒ Ⓓ Ⓔ
47. Ⓐ Ⓑ Ⓒ Ⓓ Ⓔ
48. Ⓐ Ⓑ Ⓒ Ⓓ Ⓔ
49. Ⓐ Ⓑ Ⓒ Ⓓ Ⓔ
50. Ⓐ Ⓑ Ⓒ Ⓓ Ⓔ

ALGEBRA DIAGNOSTIC TEST

This diagnostic test is designed to help you determine your strengths and your weaknesses in algebra. Follow the directions for each part and check your work.

1. The value of B in the equation $A = (h/2)(B + b)$ is:

   (A) $(2A - b)h$ (B) $2h/A - b$ (C) $2A - b$

   (D) $2A/h - b$ (E)   None of the above

2. Which of the following integers is the square of an integer for every integer x?

   (A) $x^2 + x$ (B) $x^2 + 1$ (C) $x^2 + 2x$

   (D) $x^2 + 2x - 4$ (E) $x^2 + 2x + 1$

3. Each of the integers h, m and n is divisible by 3. Which of the following integers is ALWAYS divisible by 9?
   I. hm
   II. $h + m$
   III. $h + m + n$

   (A) I only   (B) II only   (C)   III only

   (D) II and III only   (E) I, II, and III

4. What is the factorization of $x^2 + ax - 2x - 2a$?

   (A) $(x + 2)(x - a)$ (B) $(x - 2)(x + a)$ (C) $(x + 2)(x + a)$

   (D) $(x - 2)(x - a)$ (E) None of the above

5. What is the value of x in the equation

   $$\sqrt{5x - 4} - 5 = -1?$$

   (A) 2   (B) 5   (C) No value

   (D) 4   (E) -4

6. The number missing in the series, 2, 6, 12, 20, x, 42, 56 is:

   (A) 36   (B) 24   (C) 30

   (D) 38   (E) 40

7. If $T = 2\pi\sqrt{\dfrac{L}{g}}$, then L is equal to

   (A) $\dfrac{T^2}{2\pi g}$ (B) $\dfrac{T^2 g}{2\pi}$ (C) $\dfrac{T^2 g}{4\pi^2}$

   (D) $\dfrac{T^2 g}{4\pi}$ (E) $\dfrac{T^2}{4\pi^2 g}$

8. $1 + \dfrac{y}{x - 2y} - \dfrac{y}{x + 2y} =$

   (A) 0   (B) 1

   (C) $\dfrac{1}{(x-2y)(x+2y)}$ (D) $\dfrac{2x-y}{(x-2y)(x+2y)}$

   (E) $\dfrac{x^2}{(x-2y)(x+2y)}$

9. If $0 < a < 1$ and $b > 1$, which is the largest value?

   (A) $a/_b$ (B) $b/_a$ (C) $(a/_b)^2$

   (D) $(b/_a)^2$ (E) Cannot be determined

10. Given $\dfrac{(\alpha + x) + y}{x + y} = \dfrac{\beta + y}{y}$, $\dfrac{x}{y} = ?$

    (A) α/β (B) β/α (C) $\beta/\alpha - 1$

    (D) $\alpha/\beta - 1$ (E) 1

11. If n is an integer, which of the following represents an odd number?

    (A) $2n + 3$ (B) $2n$ (C) $2n + 2$

    (D) $3n$ (E) $n + 1$

12. Which of the following statements are true, if

    $x + y + z = 10$

    $y \geq 5$

    $4 \geq z \geq 3$

 I. $x < z$
 II. $x > y$
 III. $x + z \leq y$

 (A) I only   (B) II only   (C) III only

 (D) I and III   (E) I, II, and III

13. $\sqrt{X\sqrt{X\sqrt{X}}} = ?$

 (A) $X^{7/8}$ (B) $X^{7/4}$ (C) $X^{15/16}$

 (D) $X^{3/4}$ (E) $X^{15/8}$

14. If $v = \pi b^2 \left(r - {}^b/_3\right)$, then r is equal to

 (A) $\dfrac{v}{\pi b^2} + \dfrac{b}{3}$ (B) $\dfrac{v}{\pi b^2} + \dfrac{b}{3\pi}$ (C) $\dfrac{v}{\pi b^2} + 3b$

 (D) $v + \dfrac{b}{3}$ (E) $v + \dfrac{\pi b}{3}$

15. If ${}^a/_x - {}^b/_y = c$ and $xy = {}^1/_c$, then $bx = ?$

 (A) $1 - ay$ (B) ay (C) $ay + 1$

 (D) $ay - 1$ (E) $2ay$

16. If $z = x^a$, $y = x^b$ then $z^b y^a = ?$

 (A) $x^{(ab)^2}$ (B) x^{ab} (C) x^0

 (D) x^{2ab} (E) x

17. The mean (average) of the numbers 50, 60, 65, 75, x and y is 65. What is the mean of x and y?

 (A) 67   (B) 70   (C) 71

 (D) 73   (E) 75

18. If x and 10 are relatively prime natural numbers, then x could be a multiple of

    (A) 9   (B) 18   (C) 4

    (D) 25   (E) 14

19. A first square has a side of length x while the length of a side of a second square is two units greater than the length of a side of the first square. What is an expression for the sum of the areas of the two squares?

    (A) $2x^2 + 4x + 4$ (B) $x^2 + 2$ (C) $x^2 + 4$

    (D) $2x^2 + 2x + 2$ (E) $2x^2 + 3x + 4$

20. If a and b each represent a nonzero real number and if

    $$x = \frac{a}{|a|} + \frac{b}{|b|} + \frac{ab}{|ab|}$$

    the set of all possible values for x is

    (A) $\{-3, -2, -1, 1, 2, 3\}$ (B) $\{3, -1, -2\}$

    (C) $\{3, -1, -3\}$ (D) $\{3, -1\}$

    (E) $\{3, 1, -1\}$

21. If $x - y = 9$ then $3x - 3y - 1 =$

    (A) 23   (B) 24   (C) 25

    (D) 26   (E) 28

22. $4^{x-3} = \left(\sqrt{2}\right)^x$ The value of x is

    (A) 0   (B) 5   (C) 4

    (D) $\frac{1}{2}$ (E) 3

23. Find the first term of the arithmetic progression whose third term a_3 is 7 and whose eighth term a_8 is 17.

    (A) 0   (B) 2   (C) 3

    (D) 1   (E) 4

24. If $x = -2y$ and $2x - 6y = 5$ then $\dfrac{1}{x} + \dfrac{1}{y} =$

    (A) $^3/_2$　　(B) -3　　(C) -1

    (D) $-^3/_2$　　(E) 3

25. If $f(x) = 2x - 5$ then $f(x + h) =$

    (A) $2x + h - 5$　　(B) $2h - 5$　　(C) $2x + 2h - 5$

    (D) $2x - 2h + 5$　　(E) $2x - 5$

26. If $a + b = 3$ and $2b + c = 2$, then $2a - c =$

    (A) -4　　(B) -1　　(C) 1

    (D) 4　　(E) 5

27. If $x > {}^1/_5$, then

    (A) x is greater than 1.　　(B) x is greater than 5.

    (C) $^1/_x$ is greater than 5.　　(D) $^1/_x$ is less than 5.

    (E) None of the above statements is true.

28. If $f(x) = x^2 + 3x + 2$, then $[f(x + a) - f(x)]/a =$

    (A) $2x + a + 3$　　(B) $2x + 3$　　(C) $a^2 + 2ax + 3a$

    (D) $2x + a$　　(E) $(x + a)^2 - x^2$

29. If $x + 2y > 5$ and $x < 3$, then $y > 1$ is true

    (A) never.　(B) only if $x = 0$.　　(C) only if $x > 0$.

    (D) only if $x < 0$.　　(E) always.

30. If $x + y = 8$ and $xy = 6$, then $^1/_x + {}^1/_y =$

    (A) $^1/_8$　　(B) $^1/_6$　　(C) $^1/_4$

    (D) $^4/_3$　　(E) 8

31. If $x^{64} = 64$ then $x^{32} =$

    (A) 8 or -8　　(B) 12 or -12　　(C) 16

    (D) 32 or -32　　(E) 48

32. If $\sqrt{x-1} = 2$ then $(x-1)^2 =$

   (A) 4   (B) 6   (C) 8

   (D) 10   (E) 16

33. If $2^x = \dfrac{16^2 \cdot 8^3}{2^{19}}$ then $x =$

   (A) -3 (B) -2 (C) 1

   (D) 2   (E) 3

34. If $2^{(6x-8)} = 16$ then $x =$

   (A) 2   (B) 4   (C) 10

   (D) 1   (E) 6

35. $\sqrt{X\sqrt{X\sqrt{X^2}}} = ?$

   (A) X (B) $X^{7/4}$ (C) $X^{15/16}$

   (D) $X^{3/4}$ (E) $X^{15/8}$

36. The quotient of $(x^2 - 5x + 3)/(x + 2)$ is:

   (A) $x - 7 + 17/(x + 2)$ (B) $x - 3 + 9/(x + 2)$

   (C) $x - 7 - 11/(x + 2)$ (D) $x - 3 - 3/(x + 2)$

   (E) $x + 3 - 3(x + 2)$

37. If x and y are two different real numbers and $xz = yz$, then what is the value of z?

   (A) $x - y$ (B) 1   (C) x/y

   (D) y/x (E) 0

38. If $2a + 2b = 1$, and $6a - 2b = 5$, which of the following statements is true?

   (A) $3a - b = 5$ (B) $a + b > 3a - b$ (C) $a + b = -2$

   (D) $a + b < 3a - b$ (E) $a + b = -1$

39. Which of the following equations can be used to find a number n, such that if you multiply it by 3 and take 2 away, the result is 5 times as great as if you divide the number by 3 and add 2?

    (A) $3n - 2 = 5 + (n/3 + 2)$ (B) $3n - 2 = 5 (n/3 + 2)$

    (C) $3n - 2 = 5n/3 + 2$ (D) $5(3n - 2) = n/3 + 2$

    (E) $5n - 2 = n/3 + 2$

40. If $3/2 x = 5$, then $2/3 + x =$

    (A) $10/3$ (B) 4   (C) $15/2$

    (D) 8   (E) 12

41. If $x + y = 12$ and $x^2 + y^2 = 126$ then $xy =$

    (A) 9   (B) 10   (C) 11

    (D) 13   (E) 16

42. If $\dfrac{7a - 5b}{b} = 7$, then $\dfrac{4a + 6b}{2a}$ equals

    (A) $15/4$ (B) 4   (C) $17/4$

    (D) 5   (E) 6

43. The fraction

    $$\frac{7x - 11}{x^2 - 2x - 15}$$

    was obtained by adding the two fractions

    $$\frac{A}{x - 5} + \frac{B}{x + 3}.$$

    The values of A and B are:

    (A) $A = 7x, B = 11$ (B) $A = -11, B = 7x$

    (C) $A = 3, B = 4$ (D) $A = 5, B = -3$

    (E) $A = -5, B = 3$

44. What number must be added to 28 and 36 to give an average of 29?

(A) 23   (B) 32   (C) 21

(D) 4   (E) 5

45. Solve for x:

$$\frac{5}{x} = \frac{2}{x-1} + \frac{1}{x(x-1)}.$$

(A) -1 (B) 0   (C) 1

(D) 2   (E) 3

46. If $2X + Y = 2$ and $X + 3Y > 6$, then

(A) $Y \geq 2$ (B) $Y > 2$ (C) $Y < 2$

(D) $Y \leq 2$ (E) $Y = 2$

47. The expression $(x + y)^2 + (x - y)^2$ is equivalent to

(A) $2x^2$ (B) $4x^2$ (C) $2(x^2 + y^2)$

(D) $2x^2 + y^2$ (E) $x^2 + 2y^2$

48. If $x + y = 1/k$ and $x - y = k$, what is the value of $x^2 - y^2$?

(A) 4   (B) 1   (C) 0

(D) k^2 (E) $\dfrac{1}{k^2}$

49. If $3^{a-b} = 1/9$ and $3^{a+b} = 9$, then $a =$

(A) -2 (B) 0   (C) 1

(D) 2   (E) 3

50. If $\dfrac{3}{X-1} = \dfrac{2}{X+1}$, then $X =$

(A) -5 (B) -1 (C) 0

(D) 1   (E) 5

GEOMETRY
DIAGNOSTIC TEST

1. (A) (B) (C) (D) (E)
2. (A) (B) (C) (D) (E)
3. (A) (B) (C) (D) (E)
4. (A) (B) (C) (D) (E)
5. (A) (B) (C) (D) (E)
6. (A) (B) (C) (D) (E)
7. (A) (B) (C) (D) (E)
8. (A) (B) (C) (D) (E)
9. (A) (B) (C) (D) (E)
10. (A) (B) (C) (D) (E)
11. (A) (B) (C) (D) (E)
12. (A) (B) (C) (D) (E)
13. (A) (B) (C) (D) (E)
14. (A) (B) (C) (D) (E)
15. (A) (B) (C) (D) (E)
16. (A) (B) (C) (D) (E)
17. (A) (B) (C) (D) (E)
18. (A) (B) (C) (D) (E)
19. (A) (B) (C) (D) (E)
20. (A) (B) (C) (D) (E)
21. (A) (B) (C) (D) (E)
22. (A) (B) (C) (D) (E)
23. (A) (B) (C) (D) (E)
24. (A) (B) (C) (D) (E)
25. (A) (B) (C) (D) (E)

26. (A) (B) (C) (D) (E)
27. (A) (B) (C) (D) (E)
28. (A) (B) (C) (D) (E)
29. (A) (B) (C) (D) (E)
30. (A) (B) (C) (D) (E)
31. (A) (B) (C) (D) (E)
32. (A) (B) (C) (D) (E)
33. (A) (B) (C) (D) (E)
34. (A) (B) (C) (D) (E)
35. (A) (B) (C) (D) (E)
36. (A) (B) (C) (D) (E)
37. (A) (B) (C) (D) (E)
38. (A) (B) (C) (D) (E)
39. (A) (B) (C) (D) (E)
40. (A) (B) (C) (D) (E)
41. (A) (B) (C) (D) (E)
42. (A) (B) (C) (D) (E)
43. (A) (B) (C) (D) (E)
44. (A) (B) (C) (D) (E)
45. (A) (B) (C) (D) (E)
46. (A) (B) (C) (D) (E)
47. (A) (B) (C) (D) (E)
48. (A) (B) (C) (D) (E)
49. (A) (B) (C) (D) (E)
50. (A) (B) (C) (D) (E)

GEOMETRY DIAGNOSTIC TEST

This diagnostic test is designed to help you determine your strengths and your weaknesses in geometry. Follow the directions for each part and check your work.

1. An old picture has dimensions 33 inches by 24 inches. What one length must be cut from each dimension so that the ratio of the shorter side to the longer side is $^2/_3$?

   (A) $4^1/_2$ inches (B)   9 inches   (C) 6 inches

   (D) $10^1/_2$ inches (E)   3 inches

2. The greatest area that a rectangle whose perimeter is 52 m can have is

   (A) $12 \, m^2$ (B) $169 \, m^2$ (C) $172 \, m^2$

   (D) $168 \, m^2$ (E) $52 \, m^2$

3. If the triangle ABC has angle $A = 35°$ and angle $B = 85°$, then the measure of the angle x in degrees is:

   (A) 85

   (B) 90

   (C) 100

   (D) 120

   (E) 180

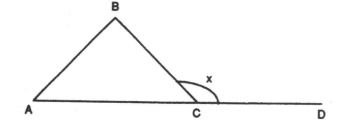

4. In the following figure, O is the center of the circle. If arc ABC has length 2π, what is the area of the circle?

   (A) 3π

   (B) 6π

   (C) 9π

   (D) 12π

   (E) 15π

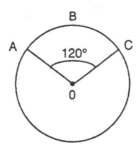

5. If the area of a rectangle is 120 and the perimeter is 44, then the length is

    (A) 30   (B) 20   (C) 15

    (D) 12   (E) 10

6. What is the measure of the angle made by the minute and hour hand of a clock at 3:30?

    (A) 60°   (B) 75°   (C) 90°

    (D) 115°   (E) 120°

7. A rectangular piece of metal has an area of 35m² and a perimeter of 24 m. Which of the following are possible dimensions of the piece?

    (A) ³⁵/₂ m × 2 m   (B) 5 m × 7 m   (C) 35 m × 1 m

    (D) 6 m × 6 m   (E) 8 m × 4 m

8. The area of ΔADE is 12 square units. If B is the midpoint of $\overline{AD}$ and C is the midpoint of $\overline{AE}$, what is the area of ΔABC?

    (A) 2 square units

    (B) 3 square units

    (C) 3¹/₂ square units

    (D) 4 square units

    (E) 6 square units

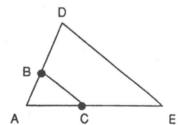

9. If the quadrilateral ABCD has angle A = 35°, angle B = 85°, and angle C = 120°, then the measure of the angle D in degrees is:

    (A) 85   (B) 90   (C) 100

    (D) 120   (E) 180

10. In the figure shown, two chords of the circle intersect, making the angles shown. What is the value of $x + y$?

    (A) 40°

    (B) 50°

    (C) 80°

    (D) 160°

    (E) 320°

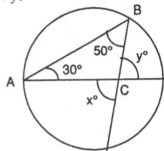

11. In the figure shown, three chords of the circle intersect making the angles shown. What is the value of θ?

    (A) 35°

    (B) 45°

    (C) 60°

    (D) 75°

    (E) 80°

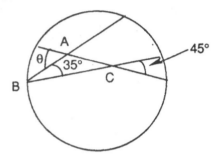

12. If a triangle of base 6 units has the same area as a circle of radius 6 units, what is the altitude of the triangle?

    (A) π   (B) 3π   (C) 6π

    (D) 12π   (E) 36π

13. The surface of a cube consists of 96 square feet. What is the volume of the cube in cubic feet?

    (A) 16   (B) 36   (C) 64

    (D) 96   (E) 216

14. If the angles of a triangle *ABC* are in the ratio of 3 : 5 : 7, then the triangle is:

    (A) acute (B) right (C) isosceles

    (D) obtuse (E) equilateral

15. If the measures of the three angles of a triangle are $(3x + 15)°$, $(5x - 15)°$, and $(2x + 30)°$, what is the measure of each angle?

    (A) 75°   (B) 60°   (C) 45°

    (D) 25°   (E) 15°

16. In the figure shown below, line l is parallel to line m. If the area of triangle ABC is 40 cm², what is the area of triangle ABD?

    (A) Less than 40 cm²

    (B) More than 40 cm²

    (C) The length of segment $\overline{AD}$ times 40 cm²

    (D) Exactly 40 cm²

    (E) Cannot be determined from the information given

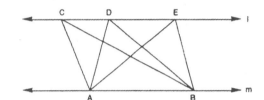

17. If the length of segment $\overline{EB}$, base of triangle EBC, is equal to $^1/_4$ the length of segment $\overline{AB}$ ($\overline{AB}$ is the length of rectangle $ABCD$), and the area of triangle EBC is 12 square units, find the area of the shaded region.

    (A) 24 square units

    (B) 96 square units

    (C) 84 square units

    (D) 72 square units

    (E) 120 square units

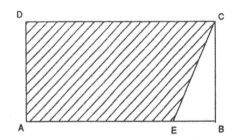

18. What is the perimeter of triangle ABC?

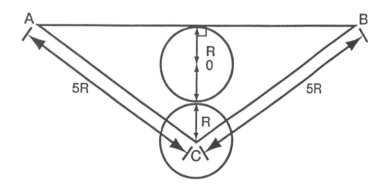

(A) $12R$ (B) $18R^2$ (C) $12R^2$

(D) $18R$ (E) $16R$

19. Which of the following alternatives is correct?

    (A) $\alpha + \beta + \gamma = 180°$

    (B) $\gamma - \alpha + 180° = \beta$

    (C) $\alpha = \beta + \gamma$

    (D) $\gamma = \alpha + \beta$

    (E) $\alpha = 180° - \beta - \alpha$

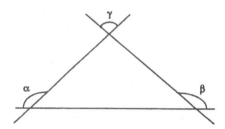

20. In the figure shown, all segments meet at right angles. Find the figure's perimeter in terms of r and s.

    (A) $r + s$

    (B) $2r + s$

    (C) $2s + r$

    (D) $r^2 + s^2$

    (E) $2r + 2s$

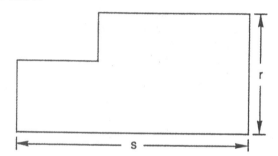

21. If lines l, m, and n intersect at point P, express $x + y$ in terms of a.

    (A) $180 - {}^a\!/_2$

    (B) ${}^a\!/_2 - 180$

    (C) $90 - {}^a\!/_2$

    (D) $a - 180$

    (E) $180 - a$

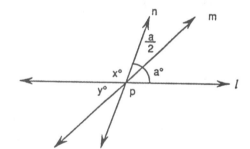

22. The measure of an inscribed angle is equal to one-half the measure of its inscribed arc. In the figure shown, triangle *ABC* is inscribed in circle *O*, and line $\overline{BD}$ is tangent to the circle at point *B*. If the measure of angle *CBD* is 70°, what is the measure of angle *BAC*?

    (A) 110°

    (B) 70°

    (C) 140°

    (D) 35°

    (E) 40°

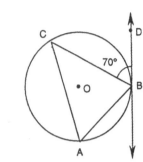

23. What is the value of *x*?

    (A) 20°

    (B) 40°

    (C) 60°

    (D) 90°

    (E) 30°

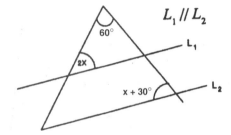

24. If the triangle *ABC* has angle *A* = 35° and angle *B* = 85°, then the measure of the angle *x* in degrees is:

    (A) 85

    (B) 90

    (C) 100

    (D) 120

    (E) 180

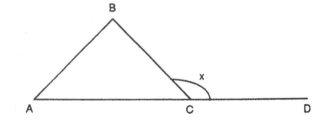

25. In the figure shown, line *r* is parallel to line *l*. Find the measure of angle *RBC*.

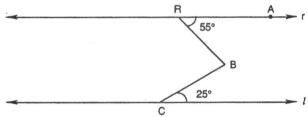

(A) 30°   (B) 80°   (C) 90°

(D) 100°   (E) 110°

26. In the five-pointed star shown, what is the sum of the measures of angles *A, B, C, D,* and *E*?

    (A) 108°

    (B) 72°

    (C) 36°

    (D) 150°

    (E) 180°

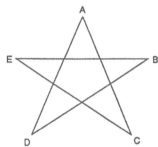

27. A room measures 13 feet by 26 feet. A rug that measures 12 feet by 18 feet is placed on the floor. What is the area of the uncovered portion of the floor?

    (A) 554 sq. ft.   (B)   216 sq. ft.   (C) 100 sq. ft.

    (D) 122 sq. ft.   (E)   338 sq. ft.

28. The area of $\triangle ADE$ is 12 square units. If *B* is the midpoint of $\overline{AD}$ and *C* is the midpoint of $\overline{AE}$, what is the area of $\triangle ABC$?

    (A) 2 square units

    (B) 3 square units

    (C) $3\frac{1}{2}$ square units

    (D) 4 square units

    (E) 6 square units

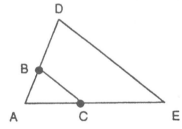

29. In $\triangle ABC$, $AB = 6$, $BC = 4$ and $AC = 3$. What kind of a triangle is it?

    (A) right and scalene   (B) obtuse and scalene

    (C) acute and scalene   (D) right and isosceles

    (E) obtuse and isosceles

30. What is the area of the shaded portion of the rectangle? The heavy dot represents the center of the semicircle.

    (A) $200 - 100\pi$ (B) $200 - 25\pi$

    (C) $30 - \dfrac{25\pi}{2}$ (D) $\dfrac{200 - 25\pi}{2}$

    (E) $\dfrac{400 - 25\pi}{2}$

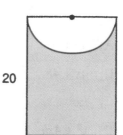

31. Find the area of the isosceles trapezoid.

    (A) $250\sqrt{3}$

    (B) 150

    (C) 250

    (D) $125\sqrt{3}$

    (E) Area cannot be found.

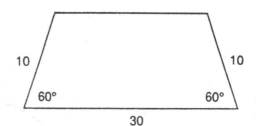

32. If the radius of a sphere is increased by a factor of 3, then the volume of the sphere is increased by a factor of

    (A) 3   (B) 6   (C) 9

    (D) 18   (E) 27

33. In the diagram shown, *ABC* is an isosceles triangle. Sides *AC* and *BC* are extended through *C* to *E* and *D* to form triangle *CDE*. The sum of the measures of angles *D* and *E* is

    (A) 150°

    (B) 105°

    (C) 90°

    (D) 60°

    (E) 30°

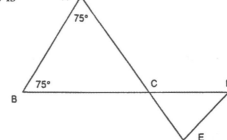

34. The box pictured has a square base with side x and a closed top. The surface area of the box is

(A) $4x + h$

(B) $4x + 4h$

(C) hx^2

(D) $x^2 + 4xh$

(E) $2x^2 + 4xh$

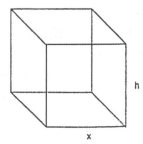

35. Quadrilaterals $ABCD$ and $AFED$ are squares with sides of length 10 cm. Arc BD and arc DF are quarter circles. What is the area of the shaded region?

(A) 50 sq. cm

(B) 100 sq. cm

(C) 80 sq. cm

(D) 40 sq. cm

(E) 10 sq. cm

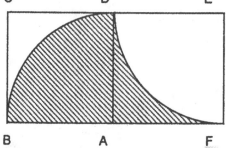

36. If the distance between two adjacent vertical or horizontal dots is 1, what is the perimeter of $\triangle ABC$? (See figure following)

(A) 5

(B) $\sqrt{3} + \sqrt{10} + \sqrt{11}$

(C) 8

(D) 9

(E) $\sqrt{2} + \sqrt{13} + \sqrt{17}$

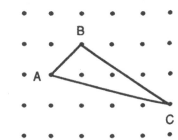

37. If the hypotenuse of a right triangle is $x + 1$ and one of the legs is x, then the other leg is

(A) $\sqrt{2x+1}$ (B) $\sqrt{2x} + 1$ (C) $\sqrt{x^2 + (x+1)^2}$

(D) 1   (E) $2x + 1$

38. The measures of the lengths of two sides of an isosceles triangle are x and $2x + 1$. Then, the perimeter of the triangle is

(A) 4x

(B) 4x +1

(C) 5x + 1

(D) 5x + 2

(E) None of the above

39. Find the length of the diagonal of the rectangular solid shown in the following figure.

(A) 7

(B) $2\sqrt{10}$

(C) $3\sqrt{5}$

(D) 11

(E) None of the above

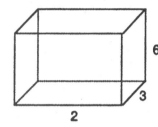

40. Find the area of the shaded portion in the following figure. The heavy dot represents the center of the circle.

(A) $100\pi - 96$

(B) $400\pi - 96$

(C) $400\pi - 192$

(D) $100\pi - 192$

(E) $256\pi - 192$

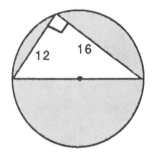

41. $m(\angle A) + m(\angle C) =$

(A) 160°

(B) 180°

(C) 190°

(D) 195°

(E) 200°

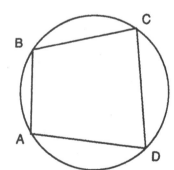

42. The area of the shaded region is:

    (A) 25 sq. units

    (B) 36 sq. units

    (C) 49 sq. units

    (D) 100 sq. units

    (E) None of the above

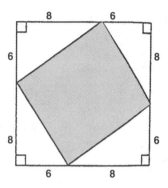

43. In the figure shown, $\triangle ABC$ is an equilateral triangle. Also, $AC = 3$ and $DB = BE = 1$. Find the perimeter of quadrilateral $ACED$.

    (A) 6

    (B) $6^1/_2$

    (C) 7

    (D) $7^1/_2$

    (E) 8

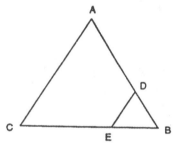

44. The sum of the exterior angles of the hexagon shown, one angle at each vertex is

    (A) 120°

    (B) 270°

    (C) 360°

    (D) 450°

    (E) None of the above

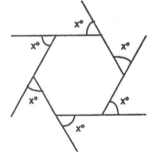

45. Find the area of the shaded region in the figure on the following page, given that $\overline{AB} = \overline{CD} = 4$ and $\overline{BC} = 8$.

(A) 40π

(B) 32π

(C) 68π

(D) 76π

(E) 36π

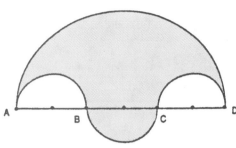

46. In the figure shown, the area of the inscribed circle is A. What is the length of a side of the square?

(A) $\sqrt{A/\pi}$

(B) $\sqrt{2A/\pi}$

(C) A/π

(D) $2\sqrt{A/\pi}$

(E) $2A/\pi$

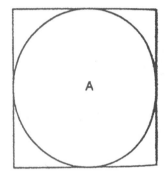

47. In the cube $ABCDEFGH$ with side $AB = 2$, what is the length of diagonal AF?

(A) 2

(B) $2\sqrt{2}$

(C) $2\sqrt{3}$

(D) 4

(E) $2\sqrt{5}$

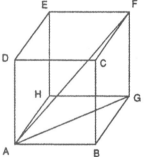

48. Find the area of the shaded region. O is the center of the given circle, whose radius is 6. The distance $\overline{AB} = 6\sqrt{2}$, the radius of a circle with its center at B.

(A) 9π

(B) 72π

(C) 18π

(D) 18π − 36

(E) 36

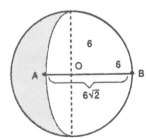

49. In the given figure, the area of the triangle *ABC* is

    (A) 65

    (B) 40

    (C) 28

    (D) 16

    (E) 14

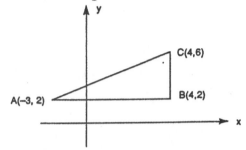

50. In the figure shown the right-angled figure is a square of length *r*, and the circular region on top of the square has radius *r*. The perimeter of the figure is

    (A) $4r + 2\pi r$

    (B) $2r + \pi r/3$

    (C) $3r + 2\pi r$

    (D) $3r + \pi r/3$

    (E) $3r + 5\pi r/3$

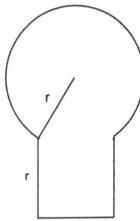

NOTES

NOTES

Level 2

¡Avancemos!

Unit 7 Resource Book

McDougal Littell

A DIVISION OF HOUGHTON MIFFLIN COMPANY

Evanston, Illinois • Boston • Dallas

Fine Art Acknowledgments

Page 87 *Remembranzas taínas* (2003), Andrés "Charlie" Simón. Oil on canvas, 40″ x 60″.
Courtesy of the artist and Samana Dreams and Quisqueya Consulting, Las Terranas, Samaná,
República Dominicana.

Page 88 Taíno artifact, AAAC/Topham/The Image Works.

Page 89 *Family Reading* (2001). Woodcut. Belkis Ramírez.

Page 90 *Paisaje, 1960* (1966), Yoryi Morel. 23.5″ x 29″. Courtesy of Colección Museo Bellapart,
Santo Domingo, República Dominicana.

ISBN-13: 978-0-618-75361-1
ISBN-10: 0-618-75361-3

2 3 4 5 6 7 8 9 - MDO- 12 11 10 09 08 07